Counseling in the Asia-Pacific Region

**Recent Titles in
Contributions in Psychology**

Counseling in the Asia-Pacific Region

Edited by
Abdul Halim Othman
and
Amir Awang

Contributions in Psychology, Number 20
Paul Pedersen, *Series Adviser*

GREENWOOD PRESS
Westport, Connecticut • London

Library of Congress Cataloging-in-Publication Data

Counseling in the Asia-Pacific region / edited by Abdul Halim Othman
and Amir Awang.
    p. cm. — (Contributions in psychology, ISSN 0736–2714 ; no. 20)
    Includes bibliographical references and index.
    ISBN 0–313–28799–6 (alk. paper)
    1. Counseling—Pacific Coast (Asia) 2. Counseling—Australasia.
I. Othman, Abdul Halim. II. Awang, Amir. III. Series.
BF637.C6C6375   1993
158′.3′095—dc20   92–45074

British Library Cataloguing in Publication Data is available.

Library of Congress Catalog Card Number: 92–45074
ISBN: 0–313–28799–6
ISSN: 0736–2714

First published in 1993

Greenwood Press, 88 Post Road West, Westport, CT 06881
An imprint of Greenwood Publishing Group, Inc.

Printed in the United States of America

The paper used in this book complies with the
Permanent Paper Standard issued by the National
Information Standards Organization (Z39.48–1984).

10 9 8 7 6 5 4 3 2 1

Contents

Foreword

If you want to know who you are and what you believe, ask the people around you who often see you more accurately and insightfully than you see yourself. That same idea applies to understanding constructs like "counseling" which have developed in the American and European cultural settings and are now familiar to most Western-educated people. While the construct label of counseling may have originated in a Euro-American envelope, the functions of counseling have been alive and healthy in every society where support, helping, facilitating, and encouraging behaviors are alive and healthy within their own indigenous contexts. This book looks at the construct "counseling" in terms of both how it has been adapted from abroad and its indigenous roots within each culture of the region. By examining counseling in the Asia-Pacific region, it will be possible to (1) obtain a more accurate and insightful understanding of the construct itself in our own cultural setting, (2) better understand the indigenous styles of support, helping, facilitating, encouraging, and people-changing skills that provide a healthy context for counseling in contrasting cultures, (3) change and adapt the constructs of counseling to our rapidly changing future needs, and (4) recognize the importance of international interdependencies for the survival and success of all.

This book seeks to develop these objectives in a variety of ways.

Each of the eight countries/cultures described in this book has a slightly different perspective on counseling. In Malaysia counseling grew out of a teaching/schooling environment to meet the problems of guidance in that setting; in Singapore it emerged from a church/religious organizational setting to deal with the welfare of troubled individuals; in Indonesia from a philosophical orientation toward sociopolitical change and the management of those dynamics among youth; in China from traditional familial thinking about power and authority relationships in the new and changing world order; in Japan from medical and clinical science as it related to progress and modernization; in Korea from a sociodevelopmental way of thinking about change and the future; in New Zealand from balancing social and economic relationships among the immigrant and indigenous populations; and in Australia from vocational choices and career planning. Counseling developed its own unique identity in each of these cultures, including both shared and unique aspects of counseling throughout the region. In the final chapter Othman and Awang summarize the issues which are an integral reason for reading this book and which may even help the reader learn something about him or herself. They discuss the importance of diversity for understanding how counseling works in the Asia-Pacific context. They describe the lack of sufficient baseline data on counseling throughout the region and the need to depend on subjective experiences and observations to understand counseling. Othman and Awang identify five major problems in the region—identity, drugs, ethics, stress, and family—and how counseling approaches these problems. They contend that the adapted notion of counseling should be integrated with indigenous perspectives about healing and cosmology. Developing counseling as a profession poses a number of difficulties which are not unique to the Asia-Pacific region.

This book provides some valuable insights into how the countries of the Asia-Pacific region adapt their networks of social support to a modernized-industrialized lifestyle of the future. In some cases these countries/cultures have independently come up with ideas and solutions that may help solve their problems better than is possible with more familiar approaches. By "fitting into" indigenous social systems outside the European-American envelope, the construct of counseling is reflected back to us in a changed and potentially improved format. The reader may learn new questions as well as new answers that will lead to a better understanding of the concepts of balance, "harmony" and cosmological unity, and subjective truth. In this way, counseling and counselors throughout the region and the world can continue to respond to the needs of a changing society.

Paul Pedersen

Preface

Recent years have witnessed a rapid development in counseling and guidance in the Asia-Pacific region, a region representing many countries and a broad spectrum of cultural traditions. Local authors have written extensively about current practices and approaches, but their works are primarily in their own native languages. Therefore, we have long had a need for a comprehensive publication in English dealing with the nature, development, and pertinent issues and problems related to counseling practice in this region. Such a work will enable us to communicate better among ourselves and with those outside the region. This book is intended to satisfy this need.

The book is a compendium of chapters written by counselors and psychologists from the countries representative of this region. All the contributors have been exposed to Western notions of counseling, and currently they are actively engaged in the development and practice of counseling in their own societies. However, they do not view counseling in the same light as when they were initially exposed. Having to face the problems and issues within their own societies where cultural traditions have seeped into all areas of human endeavor, they do not regard counseling as a static and all-embracing concept. Among the questions this book addresses are the following: what views about counseling are different from those conceptualized in the West? What strategies are adopted to suit local traditions, practices, and world views? What directions will counseling take in these societies in the future? The book seeks to reach a wide audience ranging from laypersons and students to professionals and academics interested in the development of counseling in this region.

ACKNOWLEDGMENTS

The authors would like to acknowledge the contributions of many fine individuals who have helped us tremendously over the past two years. Paul B. Pedersen first suggested the idea for this book immediately after the Second Asia-Pacific Conference on Student Affairs in Kuala Lumpur in May 1990, where about two hundred participants, including counselors, from the region attended. Later, we met some of these participants at the Association of Psychological and Educational Counselors of Asia Conference in Pulau Pinang. These initial encounters brought us together again in this volume.

Special mention must be made to my assistants, Sufiah, Nor Hamah, Azaman, Norlida, and Abdullah, who have worked tirelessly on the manuscripts. Thanks also to Wan Kader, Wan Rafaei, and Md. Shuaib who have provided us with interesting insights into counseling in our own culture. Lastly, we thank our other halves, Norlis and Aishah, who have always supported us in our endeavors.

Counseling in the Asia-Pacific Region

1. Guidance, Counseling, and Counselor Education in Malaysia

ABDUL HALIM OTHMAN
SHARIFAH BEE ABOO BAKAR

HISTORY

The history of guidance and counseling in Malaysia is closely related to the history of educational practice and problems in the schools. Since British colonial days, guidance and counseling in schools have traditionally been practiced, informally, through the system of classroom teachers, house masters, and hostel masters. In fact, according to the Federation of Malaya Annual Report on Education (1955), H. R. Cheeseman, a senior education officer in the British colonial administration, outlined the need for guidance services in the Report on Vocational Education in 1938.

Not until 1963, following the visit of R. K. MacKenzie, a Colombo Plan consultant from Canada, was a more structured guidance service introduced in the schools. A Ministry of Education report stated: "In 1963, it was decided that guidance as a specific function should be introduced in school" (1970:40). The guidance movement gained momentum when the Ministry of Education set up the Guidance and Counseling Section in the Educational Planning and Research Division (EPRD) in 1963.

The Ministry of Education then issued a circular in 1964, KP 5209/35/(4), which stressed the importance of guidance services in schools: "It has been suggested that each primary/secondary school is to appoint one guidance teacher. To ensure the effectiveness of these guidance teachers, it has been decided that they be given approximately 25 periods of academic work and be exempted from group work and other activities" (translated text).

The Guidance and Counseling Section laid the foundation for the formal introduction of guidance and counseling services in Malaysian schools. This Division (1968) conceptualized guidance as

> the assistance given to individuals in making intelligent choices and adjustments. It is based on the democratic principle that it is the duty and the right of every individual to choose his own way of life insofar as his choice does not interfere with the rights of others. The ability to make such choices is not innate, but, like other abilities, must be developed and guided. One of the functions of education is to provide opportunities for the development of such abilities. Guidance is an integral part of education and is centered directly upon this function. Guidance does not make choices for individuals. Rather, it helps them make their own choice in a way that promotes or stimulates the gradual development of the ability to make decisions independently without undue influence from others. (Ministry of Education, Malaysia 1968:1)

This definition succinctly states the advantages of guidance and counseling services in the schools.

In 1966 the Guidance and Counseling Section initiated guidance and counseling services in primary and secondary schools, and launched the idea of career teachers (Awang, 1969:12). The Division prepared school bulletins that gave explanations of guidance in primary schools, cumulative record cards, school orientation, understanding the individual child, and problems of transition to secondary schools. In the context of assisting the career teachers in secondary schools, the Guidance and Counseling Section also published and circulated a series of bulletins on career guidance

(Awang, 1969). In addition, the Section organized visits to schools to monitor the implementation of guidance and counseling services, carried out research projects, and organized seminars and exposure courses for career teachers.

Since 1973 the Schools Division has managed the task-organizing seminars and in-service courses for career and guidance teachers, but in the beginning the implementation of programs was slow owing to the lack of personnel and funds. The work of the Guidance and Counseling Unit in the Schools Division and the organization of a more comprehensive and systematic program to train guidance counselors and counseling teachers in schools gained momentum and was streamlined in 1980. In fact, in 1981, as the problems of drug abuse became more serious among students, a special officer was assigned to organize preventive drug abuse educational programs in the Unit. Courses and seminars on various aspects of guidance and counseling were organized for teachers.

STUDENT PROBLEMS

Malaysia is facing many challenges as a result of its tremendous social and economic development, technological progress, and rapid urbanization. Rapid social changes have brought with them the risk of psychosocial problems. Many individuals show syndromes of emotional disturbance, such as frustration due to unachievable goals, feelings of dissatisfaction, low self-esteem, and feelings of inferiority. Others are encountering the problems of adjustment, stress, depression, and psychological conflict.

Schools, too, suffer from the impact and influence of modernization. In schools the major psychological problems faced by adolescents are confusion in thinking, emotional turmoil, and self-conflict. According to Tan (1979),

> The major tasks the adolescent has to accomplish before achieving adult status include (a) acquiring physical maturity, (b) developing intellectual maturity, (c) preparation for a career, (d) developing

social maturity and emotional independence, (e) acquiring a value
system or a philosophy of life. Fundamental to all these developmental tasks in adolescence is the central goal of developing a
personal identity (p. 44).

In the process of balancing and adjusting to the needs of self with
the challenges of the environment, the adolescent student experiences stress and difficulties, causing anxiety and emotional conflict. Programs of a preventive and developmental nature are
needed. The individual student needs assistance to increase his or
her coping ability to face a world full of challenges. In this context,
guidance and counseling services become more important in the
schools, colleges, and universities in order to curb the psychosocial problems of adolescents.

The importance of guidance and counseling services in schools
can be gauged from the students' needs and problems. A study by
Zubir (1974) on 640 Form Four students from eight English
secondary schools in Kuala Lumpur and Petaling Jaya suggested
that students' most pressing problem was that of adjustment in
schools. Next in importance were vocational and educational
problems as they were related to the students' future well-being.

Another study by Lim and Menon (1982) on 770 male and
female Four Two and Form Four students in four secondary
schools in Selangor found that "Problems with classroom, examinations and textbooks are first, followed by problems with teaching
and learning. Problems with home and parents come next to be
followed by problems concerning themselves. Problems concerning teachers and schools are ranked 5th and 6th respectively"
(p. 14). Meanwhile, in a study on the feelings and problems of the
adolescent in three secondary schools in Peninsular Malaysia,
Chiam (1982) stressed that "More than 30% of them have feelings
of inferiority complex and lack self-confidence. 'Afraid of making
mistakes,' 'Having difficulty in making up my mind,' and 'easily
embarrassed' are also problems related to lack of self-confidence.

More than 40% of the adolescents admitted of being troubled by these problems" (p. 3).

The problems that often trouble adolescent students in Malaysia can be classified into three major categories: educational or academic problems, vocational or career problems, and personal or psycho-emotional problems.

The educational or academic problems students often confront are the problems of failure on examinations, lack of interest in education, improper techniques of studying, negative relationships with teachers, inability to make adjustments to school, inadequate knowledge about opportunities for further education, inability to concentrate, poor understanding of what has been taught, poor memory, and lack of a timetable for study.

With regard to vocational or career problems, many adolescent students are not able to state their career choices, or they postpone their choices until the public examination results are announced; they do not have an adequate knowledge about the world of work and are unaware of their abilities and potentials. In fact, many do not have concrete future plans. On the personal and psycho-emotional problems, many students have low self-esteem, experience loneliness and self-hatred, have an inability to release suppressed feelings, are unable to meet high parental expectations, lack self confidence, and face the problems of personal and family relationships. Regardless of the nature of the problems, everyone involved needs to give their immediate attention and action. In this context, teacher-counselors can play a major role in providing guidance and counseling.

In summary, guidance and counseling services can attend to the psychological welfare and the affective domain of the individual's personality, as well as the needs, values, feelings, attitudes, and aspirations of the individual. Guidance also helps create and maintain an encouraging atmosphere in the school, thereby enhancing the student's maximum potential.

THE NEED FOR TRAINED
TEACHER-COUNSELORS

Several important factors have necessitated the training of teacher-counselors in schools.

First, the abolition of the Malaysian Secondary Schools Entrance Examination in 1964 and the automatic promotion from Standard One to Form Three led to the consequent influx of students into secondary schools. Obviously, teachers have therefore had to handle students of various abilities, aptitudes, and interests.

Second, in the 1970s, drug abuse was found to occur within the adolescent group. Research carried out on 16,166 secondary school students in Selangor and Penang by the National Drug Research Center, Science University Malaysia, in 1977 showed that 11.5 percent of the students were repeat drug users. The problem of drug abuse in schools has emphasized the important role of guidance and counseling services in schools. Guidance and counseling teachers are required to organize preventive drug abuse education programs in schools.

Third, the need for guidance and counseling teachers became even more obvious with the completion of the Report of the Cabinet Committee on the Study of the Implementation of the National Education Policy in December 1979. Recommendation 239.1 of the report (Ministry of Education, Malaysia, 1979) acknowledged that career and guidance services in schools should be carried out fully. This service should also focus on counseling activities and not just on career guidance activities.

Fourth, the Guidance and Counseling Section in the Educational Planning and Research Division recommended that guidance teachers in schools be given a teaching load of twelve periods a week (Ministry of Education, Malaysia, 1982). The report also mandated that the larger secondary schools be given four guidance teachers, the large secondary schools three teachers, the medium-sized two teachers, and the small one guidance teacher. The proposal to equip every secondary school with at least one guidance teacher has obviously emphasized guidance and counseling services.

TRAINING PROGRAMS FOR
TEACHER-COUNSELORS

Historically, formal guidance and counseling services in schools began in 1963 when the Ministry of Education formulated a policy that secondary schools initiate guidance and counseling services. In 1968 the first seminar for guidance teachers in Selangor was held for three days, over three weekends. The Ministry of Education conducted the first In-Service Course in 1969. A six-day exposure course attended by 275 guidance teachers was held at the Language Institute, Kuala Lumpur, in 1969.

This activity gained momentum in October 1970, when another career and guidance seminar was held at the secondary school in Bukit Bintang. Seminars and workshops for career and guidance teachers continued with the aid of UNICEF until 1972 when the aid was terminated.

PRESERVICE TRAINING PROGRAM

The Faculty of Education in the University of Malaya has offered guidance and counseling as an elective subject in the Diploma of Education Course since 1967. Later, the Center for Educational Studies (Universiti Sains Malaysia, 1977) also offered the guidance and counseling course in their Teacher Education Training Program. Similarly, the Faculty of Education National University of Malaysia offered an elective course on guidance and counseling to students pursuing the diploma in education (Othman et al., 1981).

In 1975 the National University of Malaysia began to offer courses on guidance and counseling and vocational theory to the final-year undergraduate students in the Faculty of Social Sciences and Humanities (Othman et al., 1981). The Agricultural University of Malaysia launched the bachelor of education program (guidance and counseling) in 1981. At about the same time the Teacher Education Division (Ministry of Education, 1988) came out with a guidance and counseling curriculum, amounting to eighteen hours, as an introductory course to teacher trainees at the teacher training colleges.

IN-SERVICE TRAINING PROGRAMS

Under the in-service training programs, the Ministry of Education embarked on a number of training programs including various ad hoc courses held at various management levels, based on current needs. In-house training programs were organized and managed by key guidance and counseling personnel in schools or by the guidance and counseling resource personnel at the district and state levels.

Later, in 1980, the Teacher Education Division selected nineteen nongraduate teachers to follow a one-year specialist course in guidance and counseling at the Specialist Teacher Training College in Kuala Lumpur. These teachers were later awarded the Specialist Teaching Certificate. In 1981 another twenty teachers were selected to follow the above course, and in 1982, another forty-two were trained.

However, up to 1981 available training programs could not adequately fulfill the needs of the schools throughout the country (Lloyd, 1987). In 1982 the Teacher Education Division started an in-service guidance and counseling course (during the holidays) for trained teachers at two centers, in Kuala Lumpur and in Johore Bharu. This course received a very encouraging response. More training centers for the in-service holiday courses throughout the country were then set up. By 1984 four additional course centers had been set up. The seventh center was opened at the Malayan Teachers' Training College, Gelugor, Penang. Participants were later encouraged to attend further upgrading programs of six-months duration at the Specialist Teachers Training College, Kuala Lumpur. Upon completion of the course, participants were awarded certificates.

From the available training programs, the Ministry of Education managed to train a large number of teacher-counselors. The number of teacher-counselors trained under the one-year specialist course at the Specialist Teachers' Training College, Kuala Lumpur, between the years 1980 and 1990, totaled 269; the number trained in the in-service holiday course from seven centers was 1,249; and those trained under the six-month upgrading program totaled 264. Up to 1991, 374 teacher-counselors were trained at the bachelor's level at the Agricultural University, while 212 postgraduate teachers completed their diplomas in counseling at the National University of Malaysia (Aboo Bakar, 1991).

In spite of the rapid development of counseling and guidance in schools, no full-time counselors were appointed in public secondary schools.

COUNSELOR EDUCATION IN MALAYSIAN UNIVERSITIES

This section reviews the status of counselor education at the university level in Malaysia and discusses its prospects. It does not intend to cover counselor training institutions in the nonuniversity setting as outlined earlier. Institutions such as the Specialist Teachers Training Institute, the Prison College, and the Welfare and Home Affairs Ministries have played an important role in training counselors in Malaysia.

Scorzelli (1987a), Lloyd (1987), and Pedersen (1984) observed that counseling was a rapidly emerging profession in Malaysia and that counselor education programs mushroomed in the 1980s. The number of teacher-counselors who have continued with their guidance duties has remained low, however (Amir Awang and Latiff Mirasa, 1984).

Several factors contributed to a high dropout or noncontinuation rate among teachers trained in counseling and guidance. First, established counselor positions did not exist (they are still nonexistent) in the public schools. Second, teachers trained for counseling and guidance responsibilities continued to teach and carry out additional guidance/counseling duties in their schools. Third, when such teachers moved to other schools or were promoted, they would most likely relinquish their guidance duties. Fourth, counseling as a profession did not exist in Malaysia.

Apparently, too much lip-service was given to counseling in schools. At one point one education minister was quoted as saying that schools in Malaysia required five thousand school counselors. Given the current efforts in training, it would probably have taken more than twenty years to produce the number required, assuming that the attrition rate was at a minimum. It does appear that counseling and guidance continue to be a luxury item in Malaysian schools.

In the early 1980s a more serious attempt was made to train "counselors" for both school and nonschool settings. The drug problem in the country provided the impetus for the development of counseling at school and rehabilitation settings. Counseling was seen as a panacea for the ills of society. The training of counselors in the universities was accelerated to meet the demand: the National University of Malaysia (UKM) and the Agricultural University of Malaysia (UPM) proposed separate programs approved by the Ministry of Education. Prior to these two programs, the University of Malaya (UM) and the Science University of Malaysia (USM) conducted postgraduate courses leading to the master's in education (M.Ed.) degree in the Faculty/School of Education. Such programs, however, did not attract many candidates who aspired to be practicing counselors in schools, because the nature of such programs was research-oriented.

REPRESENTATIVE PROGRAMS

Three counselor education programs are highlighted in this chapter, for they represent three different emphases.

The University of Malaya

The University of Malaya, established in 1959, has offered research degrees in guidance and counseling at the master's and doctorate levels since the late 1960s. Although the degree program has been primarily research-oriented, it has recently become sensitive to new needs and demands, suggesting certain changes.

According to Salim (1988), the new program was to prepare qualified secondary school teachers with professional skills and experiences for entry into secondary school counseling positions. The program recruited qualified and experienced graduate teachers and was provided with a comprehensive counselor education program leading to a master's degree in education. The program, requiring more than one year's preparation, was divided into two parts: academic on-campus counselor education experiences and the in-school practicum or internship experiences and research.

The typical individual entering the program was expected to have a strong background in education. The counselor preparation experiences in the first part encompassed the following substantive areas: Foundation of Guidance and Counseling; Career Development and Use of Information in Guidance; the Process of Interpersonal Relations in Guidance and Theories and Techniques of Counseling; Measurement; Evaluation and Research in Guidance; Consultation; and Practicum.

The practicum was designed to provide a closely supervised experience of actual counseling with secondary school students. Practicum experiences were built around an individual student's growth and development, which has been a result of other aspects of the program. Practicum experience was provided in two settings: actual school settings and the counseling laboratory. The second part of the program involved in-school practicum/internship or conducting research and the submission of a written report on the practicum/internship or thesis.

The National University of Malaysia

The first counselor education program in the university started in the Department of Psychology. This program has a broad focus, beginning at the diploma through the master's/doctoral levels. The counselor education program in the department has its roots in the university's ten-year (1978–1987) master plan (Universiti Kebangsaan Malaysia, 1978). Othman, Rahman, and Yusof (1983) claimed that the diploma program in the university was designed to produce committed and competent counselors with a strong foundation of psychological and related knowledge. Counseling was considered an applied area of psychology. Four major elements were incorporated in the counselor education curriculum: philosophical, theoretical, empirical, and methodological and practical. Courses in the diploma program were divided into two categories: the core and the electives.

Core courses include Principles of Guidance and Counseling; Theories of Counseling; Theories of Career Development; Personality; Basic Skills and Techniques of Counseling; Research Methodology; Statistics; Psychology for Professional Groups; Behavior Modification; Seminar in Substance Abuse; Pre-practicum in Counseling; and Practicum in Counseling. The elective courses include selected courses from the Department of Psychology or courses from other faculties. The core courses comprise thirty units (equivalent to thirty credit hours) from a total of thirty-seven units (credit hours), to be completed in one calendar year. The practicum comprised nine units lasting about ten weeks (260 practicum hours). The practicum requires a mini-research project and counseling practice. Pedersen (1984), an external examiner from Syracuse University, reported that the research projects done were of high quality; many used sophisticated statistical analyses in their methodologies. Scorzelli (1987a), a Fulbright professor at the National University of Malaysia in 1986, reported that the diploma in psychology (counseling) program was the most developed counseling program.

From the beginning the diploma program was designed for experienced teachers with a minimum of three years of postgraduate teaching experience. Most of them have assumed counseling responsibilities in schools or as lecturers in teacher training colleges. The past six years have witnessed an influx of officers from other ministries and government agencies enrolling in the counseling program. (See Table 1.1.) As part of the requirement for the diploma, students are required to conduct research relevant to counseling. To date, there are 379 research projects encompassing many areas in the field of counseling and psychology.

Pedersen (1984) observed that the "research projects tend to focus on original research in a scope that is probably beyond the ordinary grasp of diploma level students, and theses written by former students are of high quality with more recent theses being somewhat more sophisticated than the earlier ones." He also noted that in some areas the theses demonstrated sophisticated statistical and methodological skills.

Evaluation of the Program. A number of evaluation studies were carried out on the diploma program and the graduates of the program. One study (Jaafar, 1981) was conducted on the graduates of the program one year after the program was completed. It was found that between 60 and 70 percent of the graduates were conducting counseling-related activities in their schools. Other studies (Arshad, 1984; Jonid, 1983) found that the teachers and administrators viewed the diploma graduates positively and that the program was successful in training "good and reliable counselors."

Evaluation reports by external examiners suggested changes and adaptations to the current program. Pedersen (1984) for instance, suggested that the diploma should be a practical certificate and clearly distinguishable from the master's degree. Then it follows that the diploma may need to modify its structure toward

Table 1.1
Background of Students in the Diploma in Psychology (Counseling) UKM, 1980–1993

SESSION	MINISTRY OF EDUCATION	WELFARE MINISTRY	SPORTS & YOUTH MINISTRY	PRISON DEPT.	HOME AFFAIRS/ POLICE FORCE	PUBLIC SERVICE DEPT.	RELIGIOUS AFFAIRS DEPT.
1980/81	39						
1981/82	47						
1982/83	25	4	2		1		
1983/84	22	3		2			
1984/85	21			5			
1985/86	21	4		1	4		1
1986/87	13	1	1	3	2	1	
1987/88	13			7	3	1	
1988/89	12			3	5	1	
1989/90	8	1		7	3		1
1990/91	18			3	6	2	2
1991/92	13			3	4	1	3
1992/93	14	3		2	5	1	3
TOTAL	226	16	3	36	33	7	10

HIGHER EDUCATION	CITY HALL	FAMILY PLANNING BOARD	DEFENSE MINISTRY	HEALTH MINISTRY	OTHER	TOTAL
						39
						47
		1				33
						27
						26
1				1		33
1	1					23
	1				1	26
1				1	1	24
1	2		3		3	29
	1		1		3	36
	2		2	1	5	34
	3		4			35
4	10	1	10	3	13	412

Note: The "Other" category includes MARA, SEDC, Voluntary Organizations, and Foreign Countries.

Source: Department of Psychology, National University of Malaysia (UKM).

graduates in both school and nonschool settings. It was also suggested that the graduates from the diploma program would need continuing support from the university to help them strengthen the identity of counselors, thus increasing the recognized status of diploma students.

The Agricultural University of Malaysia

This university offers a four-year bachelor's degree in the Faculty of Educational Studies. The major objective of the program is to train competent guidance teachers for secondary schools (Hashim, 1988).

Four major elements of the bachelor of education (guidance and counseling) program were:

1. Knowledge of, and issues in, guidance and counseling, human behavior, and theoretical approaches
2. Basic counseling skills
3. Individual and group experiences
4. Supervised practical work and research

The four-year basic degree program in guidance and counseling requires 136 credit hours in counseling, guidance, psychology, sociology, education, statistics, research, language courses, and minor and elective courses. Students are primarily teachers who have obtained the Certificate of Education and have attended courses in guidance and counseling either at the Specialist Teachers Training Institute or other courses conducted by the Ministry of Education.

One study conducted on the first graduates of the program (Hashim, 1988) showed that too much emphasis was placed on the theoretical aspects of guidance and counseling and that thirteen teachers identified themselves as guidance and counseling teachers compared to twenty-two who called themselves teachers first, while the majority (69 percent) preferred a combination of guidance and counseling with teaching.

THE MASTER'S AND PH.D. PROGRAMS

Four universities in Malaysia offer graduate programs at the master's and Ph.D. levels: the University of Malaya, the National University of Malaysia, the Agricultural University of Malaysia, and the Science University of Malaysia. All programs are intended to train qualified guidance and counseling teachers for positions in schools or teacher training colleges. However, there is a heavy emphasis on research, resulting in neglect of the practicum or practical experiences in counseling.

The number of students graduating with a master's in guidance and counseling is still insignificant. The future of these programs lies in the amount and nature of course work offered where candidates would be expected to follow systematic course work, supervised skills practice, and project work somewhat similar to the diploma program of the National University of Malaysia or the bachelor of education (guidance and counseling) program of the Agricultural University of Malaysia.

ISSUES AND PROBLEMS IN COUNSELOR EDUCATION IN MALAYSIA

The major issues and problems confronting counseling and counselor education in Malaysia are much the same as those faced by other societies that attempt to implement foreign ideas and experiences. Although counseling is strictly an American enterprise and has readily found its way across the Atlantic and the Pacific, implementation of the counseling ideas, principles, and practices has led to uncertainties, dilemmas, and roadblocks. Apart from the basic cultural differences that exist, traditions, political ideologies, religion, and level of technological and economic development present problems that are not easily surmountable.

The field of counseling is in its infancy in Malaysia, as are other fields in the human service professions such as psychology, psychiatry, and social work. The immediate problem is related to professional identity. In countries where counseling has advanced both theoretically and professionally, the field has found itself a niche in the academic and professional institutions. In Malaysia, counseling has yet to establish itself in these institutions. Currently, several models appear in Malaysia (Lloyd, 1987). In one institution, counseling established itself within the field of psychology, while in another, counseling found its place in education. Perhaps this is an extension of the problems experienced in Western countries where the counselor educators were trained. One way to resolve this issue is for counseling to establish its own identity. It would be easier for counseling in Malaysia to establish its own identity because it has not yet been involved in legal, financial, and political issues.

Another related issue involves training where various levels of competency are required in different settings. It is often believed and argued that counselor trainees do not need lengthy academic preparation before they can be considered competent to do counseling. In this view, counseling is regarded as a human encounter, requiring less technical knowledge and skills than is required of technologists. The human component in counseling is often considered more important than the technical and knowledge components. As a result, some planners consider training counselors outside the universities. In Malaysia, counselors are trained at various levels, ranging from a four-year academic institution to nondegree-granting two-year institutions. This is perhaps a temporary arrangement owing to the great demand for school counselors. As the situation changes, school counselors should also be expected to have a longer academic preparation, perhaps at the postgraduate degree.

Counselors trained in a foreign country must learn to apply their skills and attitudes to their own social and cultural milieu. Their assumptions about their clients, their clients' problems, and their clients' situations are colored by the assumptions the counselors acquired in their own training. They bring to bear some "hidden scenario" to their clients. This is probably a major problem facing Western-trained Malaysian counselors in dealing with indigenous clients. It is necessary to set up more local training institutions with a multicultural focus.

Counseling has not achieved professional status in Malaysia, unlike the situation in some Western countries. The professional standards required to prepare counselors have to be formulated by a strong professional association. Although the Association of Malaysian Counseling (PERKAMA) has been established, it is only a loose body that does not limit its membership to qualified or certified counselors, for Malaysia has no legal "umbrella" covering the status of counselors. Anyone can claim to be a counselor, regardless of preparation and competency. Perhaps, then, the professional status of counselors in this country should be upgraded, with the proper backing of the Malaysian Parliament.

COUNSELOR EDUCATION AND RESEARCH OUTPUT

Research in counseling and guidance in Malaysia is in its infancy. The number of studies relating to psychological phenomena is increasing through a concerted effort by the Department of Psychology, and Faculty of Education (UKM), the Department of Education (UPM), the Department of Pedagogy and Educational Psychology (UM), and the Center for Educational Studies (USM).

Othman (1984a) reviewed eighty studies related to counseling conducted by students at UKM. The studies were carried out in partial fulfillment of degree or diploma requirements. He found that the studies were still exploratory in nature, with a greater emphasis on vocational guidance and psychology, and that few studies in counseling employed the quasi-experimental methodology and testing or evaluation of outcomes. He concluded that "we are still in the dark (empirically speaking) with regard to counseling and guidance in Malaysia."

Lloyd (1986) attempted to answer the two basic questions pertaining to research in counseling and guidance in Malaysia: (1) "Do the guidance and counseling journal articles published in Malaysia tend to cite references to writing originating in the United States and the United Kingdom more so than references to writing originating in Malaysia?" and (2) "Have the guidance and counseling journal articles produced in Malaysia tended to become less dependent upon foreign references during the more recent years" (p. 31)? His data were based on ten journals produced in Malaysia covering the period 1958–1984. The review showed that 204 references were from the United States, while 177 references were from Malaysia. Few references were made to publications from the United Kingdom. Lloyd also found that the references in the guidance and counseling articles shifted away from foreign sources at two reference points: before 1980 (28 local and 169 foreign) and after 1980 (149 local, 89 foreign). He attributed this trend to the increasing volume of writing in Malaysia, particularly in Bahasa Malaysia (Malay language), the increasing number of counseling and guidance graduates trained locally, and the greater confidence of Malaysian counselors in the status of the counseling profession.

Any researcher attempting to conduct studies on guidance and counseling in Malaysia in this early stage would have to overcome several problems or risk inconclusive or uninterpretable results. One problem is that of "cultural leap" or "leap frog" in cross-cultural research, as a number of authorities in the field have often pointed out. Berry (1968) suggested that the following factors be considered in cross-cultural studies:

1. Considering the purpose of cross-cultural methodology
2. Obtaining a comparable standard in the groups studied
3. Using cultural groups that are really different

4. Obtaining the number of groups required in order to arrive at a valid interpretation

Pedersen (1984) recommended that "the validation of psychological test measures and research methods in the Malaysian context would be helpful to the students using those tests in research . . . this would further help to indigenize the practical relevance of psychology and increase the usefulness of the field as perceived locally." He also suggested making research efforts through replication studies, co-authored research with scholars in other countries, and the development of a cross-cultural emphasis.

By 1988 research carried out in counselor education programs in the four Malaysian universities had attempted to recognize observations made by Pedersen (1984), Othman (1984a), and Lloyd (1986). An increasing interest in research on counseling and guidance has also been shown not only among academics but also among professionals outside the academic setting. The number of studies carried out by the two institutions offering counseling degrees and diplomas totaled 252, with 61 percent done at the National University of Malaysia and 38.9 percent at the Agricultural University of Malaysia. Quantitatively, it appears that the two institutions were moving rapidly toward accumulating an important database on counseling and guidance in Malaysia.

CONCLUSION

The field of counseling and guidance found its place in Malaysia as a result of rapid socioeconomic, cultural, and technological changes and progress. The development of counseling and its acceptability as a human service provider gained impetus after drugs became a major problem. Many people consider counseling to be a panacea for social evils such as drug addiction, delinquency, and indiscipline in schools. As a result, counselor education and training programs were established in university and nonuniversity settings. Very often, this enthusiasm about training counselors ignored the fact that it was also necessary to carefully evaluate the effectiveness of counseling as conceptualized and practiced in the West. If counseling is to be developed meaningfully in Malaysia, there is an urgent need for continuous research and evaluation of Western models. Counselor education programs in Malaysia require continuous reevaluation if they are to be developed further. Current issues pertaining to counseling and counselor education must be immediately addressed. Finally, counselor educators and professional counselors must dedicate their efforts to producing a multicultural framework.

REFERENCES

Arshad, Faidzah. (1984). Perkembangan dan penilaian program latihan Diploma Kaunseling di UKM [The development and evaluation of a diploma in counseling program at UKM]. Unpublished Honours Thesis, UKM, Bangi.

Awang, Amir. (1969). *A Survey of Guidance Services to Malaysian Primary and Secondary Schools As Provided by the Educational Planning and Research Division, Ministry of Education, Malaysia and Some Suggestions for their Progress.* Kuala Lumpur: University of Malaya.

Awang, Amir, and Mirasa, Latiff. (1984). Guidance and counseling in Malaysian schools. A review and critique. In *Proceedings of Third Asian Workshop on Child and Adolescent Development.* Vol. 2, pp. 1–18. Kuala Lumpur: Universiti Malaya.

Bakar, Sharifah Bee Aboo. (1991). Kajian Program Latihan Bimbingan Dan Kaunseling Dalam Perkhidmatan (Kursus Dalam Cuti) Di Maktab Perguruan Persekutuan Pulau Pinang [A study of in-service guidance and counseling training (holiday courses) at the Pulau Pinang Federal Teacher's College]. Published M.Ed. diss., University of Malaya, Kuala Lumpur.

Berry, J. W. (1968). On cross-cultural comparability. *International Journal of Psychology*, 4, 119–128.

Chiam, H. K. (1987). Adolescents in Malaysia. Paper presented at Seminar Education for Peace, Human Understanding and Development, World Organization of Scout Movement, Kuala Lumpur, Malaysia.

Federation of Malaya Annual Report on Education for 1955. (1955). Kuala Lumpur: Art Printing Work.

Hashim, Aminah Haji. (1988). Report on an evaluation study of UPM bachelor of education (guidance and counseling) graduates. Unpublished manuscript.

Humphreys, J. A., Traxler, A. E., and North, R. D. (1960). *Guidance Services*. Chicago: Science Research Associates, Inc.

Jaafar, Badariah. (1981). Peranan dan fungsi graduan-graduan Diploma Kaunseling lulusan UKM [The roles and functions of diploma in counseling graduates]. Unpublished Diploma Project UKM, Bangi.

Jackson, R., and Juniper, D. F. (1971). *A Manual of Educational Guidance*. London: Holt, Rinehart and Winston Ltd.

Jonid, Rosini. (1983). Penilaian terhadap program latihan Diploma Kaunseling [An evaluation of a diploma in counseling training program]. Unpublished Honours Thesis, UKM, Bangi.

Leong, Y. C., Chiam, H. K., and Chew, S. M., eds. (1984). *Proceedings of the Workshop on Preparation for Adulthood. Third Asian Workshop on Child and Adolescent Development, 9–14 April 1984*. Kuala Lumpur: Faculty of Education, University of Malaya.

Lim, H. K., and Menon, S. (1982). Socio-psychological perspectives on students in four secondary schools in Selangor. In *Persidangan Nasional Mengenai Kaum Remaja*. Kuala Lumpur: Utusan Publications & Distributors Sdn. Bhd.

Lloyd, A. (1986). The sources of citations for guidance and counseling articles. *Jurnal PERKAMA*, 2, 29–38.

Lloyd, A. (1987). Counselor Education in Malaysia. *Counselor Education and Supervision*, 26 (3), 221–227.

Ministry of Education, Malaysia. (1963). *Guidance Services*. Kuala Lumpur: Kementerian Pelajaran, Malaysia.

Ministry of Education, Malaysia. (1964). Perlantikan Guru Bimbingan, KP/5209/35/(4) [Appointment of guidance teachers]. (Circular Bahagian Perancangan dan Penyelidikan Pelajaran).

Ministry of Education, Malaysia. (1968). *Outline of Guidance Services*. Kuala Lumpur: Bahagian Perancangan dan Penyelidikan Pelajaran.

Ministry of Education, Malaysia. (1970). *Education in Malaysia*. Kuala Lumpur: Dewan Bahasa Dan Pustaka.

Ministry of Education, Malaysia. (1976). *Surat Pekeliling Ikhtisas Bil. 5/1976: Kemudahan Bilik Untuk Perkhidmatan Panduan Pelajaran dan Kerjaya, KP(BS) 8548/1/Vol. II/(49)* [Room facilities for education and career guidance services]. (Surat Pekeliling Bahagian Sekolah-Sekolah).

Ministry of Education, Malaysia. (1979). *Report of the Cabinet Committee: To Review the Implementation of the Education Policy.* Kuala Lumpur: Berita Publishing Sdn. Bhd.

Ministry of Education, Malaysia. (1982). *Pindaan Kepada Pekeliling Pentadbiran Bilangan 3/1967, KP(PP) 0050/117/(58)* [Amendments to Circular No 3/1967], *20 Mei 1982.* (Circular Bahagian Perjawatan dan Perkhidmatan).

Ministry of Education, Malaysia. (1988). *Sukatan Pelajaran Ilmu Pendidikan: Kursus Pendidikan Perguruan Asas* [The education syllabus—basic teacher training course]. Kuala Lumpur: Bahagian Pendidikan Guru.

Newsome, A., Thorne, B. J., and Wyld, K. L. (1973). *Student Counseling in Practice.* London: University of London Press Ltd.

Othman, Abdul Halim. (1983). The training of counselors at UKM. Symposium Paper at the Third Asian Regional Conference of the IACCP: UKM Bangi.

Othman, Abdul Halim. (1984a). Penyelidikan Kaunseling dan Bimbingan di Malaysia: Satu penerokaan di sebuah institusi pengajian tinggi [Research in counseling and guidance in Malaysia: explorations in an institution of higher education]. *Jurnal PERKAMA*, 1, 122–139.

Othman, Abdul Halim. (1984b). Peranan kaunselor di sekolah dalam konteks perubahan masyarakat [The role of school counselors in the context of societal changes]. *Majallah Psikologi*, 5, 44–50.

Othman, Abdul Halim, Rahman, Wan Rafaei Abdul, and Yusof, Aminuddin. (1983). An evaluation of the first diploma in counseling program at the Universiti Kebangsaan Malaysia. *Akademika*, 23, 83–95.

Othman, Abdul Halim, and Rahman, Wan Rafaei Abdul. (1987). Issues and problems related to the teaching of psychology and training of psychologists. *The Role of Universities in Developing Nations.* Bangi: UKM.

Othman, Abdul Halim, Rahman, Wan Rafaei Abdul, and Nasir, Rohany. (1981). *Kaunseling Dan Kerjaya.* Kertas kerja yang dibentangkan di Seminar Psikologi Dan Masyarakat Ke-2, April 20–23, 1981, Universiti Kebangsaan Malaysia, Bangi.

Pedersen, P. (1984). Final report by the External Examiner to the Vice-Chancellor of Universiti Kebangsaan Malaysia. Unpublished report.

Salim, Suradi. (1987). Personal communication.

Scorzelli, J. F. (1987a). Counseling in Malaysia: An emerging profession. *Journal of Counseling and Development*, 65, 238–240.

Scorzelli, J. F. (1987b). Counselor education in Malaysia: A need for a rehabilitation specialisation. *Jurnal Perkama*, 2, 53–58.

Staff. (January 9, 1983). Full time counselors. *New Sunday Times*, p. 12.

Tan, T. H. (1979). Emotional problems of adolescents. *Jernal Panduan MAVOGA*, 1, 39–45.

Universiti Kebangsaan Malaysia. (1978). Perancangan Universiti Kebangsaan Malaysia 1978–1987. [Master Plan for the National University of Malaysia 1978–1987]. Bangi Malaysia: Universiti Kebangsaan Malaysia.

Universiti Sains Malaysia. (1977). Buku Panduan Pusat Ilmu Pendidikan 1977/78 [Handbook of The Center for Educational Studies 1977/78]. Pulau Pinang: Universiti Sains Malaysia.

Zubir, Rohana. (1974). Perception of Adolescent Problems by Teachers and Their Pupils Selected from Four English Medium Secondary School in Kuala Lumpur and Petaling Jaya. Unpublished M.Ed. diss., University of Malaya, Kuala Lumpur.

2. Counseling in Singapore: Development and Trends

ANTHONY YEO

Singapore is at the same stage in counseling as most other Asian nations. Only in 1964 was counseling as we understand it introduced into Singapore. At that time the country had no counseling centers, no private psychiatrists, and only a couple of qualified psychologists. As a result, a group of doctors, pastors, missionaries, and other concerned people got together and proposed the establishment of a counseling center to offer help to those with emotional distress. Most members of this group were associated primarily with the church. Subsequently, some professionals from the United States visited Singapore and offered ideas on how to set up a counseling service as a pilot project providing help from a Methodist church. This project was launched in 1966 under the direction of the late Reverend Dr. Gunner Teilman.

This project was known as the Churches' Counseling Centre until 1975 when it was named the Counseling and Care Centre, to reflect its attempt to be a community service for all people. During the first ten years, the center was staffed primarily by professionals from the United States, most of whom were pastoral psychologists/ counselors. The establishment of the Churches' Counseling Centre provided the impetus for development of other services. The Samaritans of Singapore (SOS), a telephone suicide prevention service, was organized in 1969 through the center. Subsequently, the Singapore Association for Mental Health was initiated, and it continues as a mental health agency in Singapore. Since then there has been a steady growth and development of counseling services through religious institutions, social welfare agencies, the military, schools, colleges, and universities. Drug counseling also became important beginning in 1976.

With the introduction of pastoral care and guidance programs in schools, counseling has become an acceptable way to deal with stress. It is also being introduced to industries, with supervisors and managers being trained to apply counseling skills for effective management.

While counseling was developing in Singapore, only minimal effort was made to provide training in counseling at institutions of higher learning. A degree program in social work has been in place for many years, but the psychology program was introduced only in 1986 at the National University of Singapore. Previously, anyone wishing to train in psychology had to go overseas. For some time, the only available training in counseling was the social work program, the clinical pastoral education program offered for pastors, and pastoral counseling courses offered through the Trinity Theological College and Churches' Counseling Center.

The situation is different now, even though there is still no formal degree program in counseling. Counseling is taught as a course in the universities and colleges as part of social work, psychology, education, and pastoral training programs. The formal programs are currently offered by the Counseling and Care Centre, a nongovernment mental health agency. (These programs are described later in this chapter.)

APPROACHES TO COUNSELING

When counseling was introduced to Singapore, it was strongly oriented toward the psychodynamic and nondirective models. It also took on a medical model, with primary focus on the individual and intrapsychic forces. Much of the counseling was slanted toward the pastoral approach since missionary pastors were the pioneers in the field. Marriage and family counseling became equally important as people were beginning to open up to such a service. However, the focus was almost always on the individual, even though it was known as marriage and family counseling. Among the various approaches that became important were behavioral techniques, group counseling or encounter groups, transactional analysis, and reality therapy. Recently, the family systems approach or family therapy has become important in Singapore.

When we survey the situation today, it is difficult to identify a prominent approach or style that is commonly practiced by counselors. Indeed, a rather varied experimental pattern is emerging. Whatever seems to be of value can find its place among counselors in Singapore. Nonetheless, some emerging trends are becoming apparent, especially with the formation of some professional counseling associations and the introduction of family and marital therapy training. These trends are highlighted in a later section of this chapter.

ENCOUNTER WITH WESTERN MODELS

Counseling was introduced to Singapore by Westerners familiar with Western modes of thinking and counseling practices. It was inevitable then that counseling practice would be Western oriented. Although Singaporeans are fairly influenced by the West in many ways, they are still Asians. They would naturally respond to Western approaches as Asians, and that seems to have highlighted some difficulties for counselors and counseling practice. The following characteristics of counseling are currently presenting problems in Singapore:

Nondirective Position. The nondirective approach requires that the counselor be reflective, client centered, and facilitative without directing. Such a posture demands that the counselor be passive, giving the client maximum opportunity to verbalize. This approach is helpful inasmuch as attending behavior is demonstrated to engage the client in counseling. Unfortunately, this is not enough, for most clients expect counselors to be active and directive. They also expect to talk to a counselor who is older and wiser and who can give specific advice. In reality, however, the majority of counselors are not very old, even though they may be wise enough. Adopting a client-centered posture is helpful up to a point. If counselors do not direct, clients may question their credibility and be disappointed that nothing more concrete is being offered besides listening.

Focus on Feelings. Singaporeans generally are not verbally expressive, for, traditionally, to express feelings is often regarded as a sign of weakness. Control is encouraged. With its tendency to focus on feelings, people treated counseling with some reservations, finding it difficult to relate at the feeling level and preferring to rationalize.

Direct Approach. Counseling in the Western mode tended to involve clients in open confrontation. Clients are encouraged to talk freely, especially in marriage and family counseling situations, and to engage in open communication. Confrontation is often involved, with minimal regard for privacy and respect for hierarchy in the family. This approach may conflict with the Singaporean traditions of appropriate behavior between children and parents, husband and wife.

Group Counseling or Group Work. This is usually practiced independently of consideration for family relationships. Individualism is encouraged, and the permissive atmosphere of the group often promotes behavior that could be disruptive in the family. Some group experiences lead to physical contact, a behavior that is not usually expressed openly, except among the younger generation.

Focus on Individual and Intrapsychic Forces. This characteristic is normally neglectful of the client's systemic and family relationship. Counseling tends to focus on self-actualization and self-development, an emphasis that has unwittingly led to a mode of thinking that is individualistic and even self-centered. Minimal consideration is frequently given to how other people are affected by an individual's problems.

An Asian is a member of a family, a community. By focusing on the individual, the counselor may either alienate him from the family or contribute to disruptive behavior. The individual would need to relate to other systems in society, and whatever intervention is planned, these relationships must be considered.

Assertiveness Training.   Traditionally, a Singaporean is taught to show regard for others, preferably at the expense of oneself. Assertiveness has also been equated with aggression. To assert oneself could mean being self-centered without due regard for others. Although nonassertiveness is not encouraged, whatever assertiveness training is advocated must be properly modified to avoid negative consequences for the person and his or her relationships.

Counselors, having adopted Western approaches, have had to adapt them to local situations. Most of the methods have not presented a great deal of difficulties, for counseling technology as such can be easily transferred to the Singaporean situation without causing any problems. However, as noted above, these approaches cannot be used indiscriminately without giving careful attention to local cultures and behavior. Until indigenous models are developed, counselors will have to contextualize Western counseling models to make them relevant and useful.

The Current State of Counseling

When we examine the state of counseling in Singapore, three aspects are notable. The first concerns counseling as part of the mental health provision, the second deals with the professional practice of counseling, and the third, the training of counselors.

Counseling Services.   Counseling was originally regarded as a Western idea that was meant solely for those who were either weak or mentally disturbed. Since it is rooted in psychoanalysis and the treatment of psychological disturbance, a stigma was attached to those who sought counseling. This view is rapidly changing with

urbanization and technological advancement. The effects of change
have been felt in all sectors of life. Family ties are weakening and
with liberalization of thinking and lifestyle, people are turning
from traditional sources of help to outside agencies.

Most mental health agencies report a steady increase in the
number of clients seeking help in recent years. In 1991, the
Samaritans of Singapore (SOS), a telephone suicide prevention
service, handled 24,266 callers who called for help. This represents
a vast increase from 19,648 in 1981. The Counseling and Care
Centre saw 3,261 clients in 1990 compared to 469 in 1970. There
has also been an increase in the provision of mental health services.
In 1966 when the Counseling and Care Centre started operations,
it was the only known mental health agency. In 1991 over fourteen
hotline counseling services were recorded, more than ten counseling agencies were registered, and many informal services were
offered by religious and civic organizations. Counseling has also
become an established part of the education system, with the
introduction of the pastoral care and guidance program in schools.
Almost every school has a teacher designated to provide counseling to students, and all teachers are expected to undergo some form
of training to respond in a caring manner to them.

The extent of growth in counseling is also seen in the formal
provision of such a service in both the military and industries.
Military personnel are covered by the Singapore Armed Forces
Counseling Service, whereas in the commercial sector special
stress management programs and counseling services have been
instituted to help employees cope with the pressures of life both at
work and at home.

One of the most widely accepted areas of counseling is in the
treatment of drug abusers. In the early 1970s drug counseling
began to gain prominence. A report on the outcome of counseling
indicated a lower relapse rate (56.4 percent) among those who
underwent counseling. There was a substantially higher rate
(82.2 percent) among those who refused counseling (*Sunday Times*,
1992). These developments indicate a clear acceptance of counsel-

ing, even though pockets of the population may still be resistant to it. This acceptance could be attributed to the influence of the media and a society that is increasingly becoming more psychological in its orientation. The fact that most of these services are offered as welfare provisions without charge could be another factor in facilitating their wide acceptance. Counseling and psychotherapy as a fee-paying service is still a new idea to many. Being a professional counselor or therapist in a private practice remains a very new idea.

The Counseling Profession.   Counseling as a distinct discipline is still in its early stage of development. This is rather unfortunate given the fact that counseling was formally introduced in 1966. Counseling is an activity practiced by people from all walks of life. It is still regarded merely as advice giving that could be done by anyone with something to offer.

In 1983 the Singapore Association for Counseling (SAC) was established to provide a common professional base for the advancement of counseling in Singapore. With this event came an attempt to identify counseling as a profession. Although anyone could identify him or herself as a counselor, the SAC helps to distinguish a professional from a nonprofessional. It has also adopted a code of ethics for professional practice to ensure that counselors maintain appropriate professional conduct.

One of the concerns for professional development has to do with the status and remuneration of counselors. Most counselors are employed in the social service sector. As such, salaries are normally not commensurate with those of other professionals. There are still not enough positions for counselors, as a result of which many are employed in other capacities with counseling as a secondary function. Unlike their counterparts in the United States, nonmedical mental health professionals do not have clear legal status. No counselor is required to be licensed in order to practice, nor does a counselor need proper training to hold a position in the field.

While counselors have been strengthening their professional

image, their practice has been taking on a more definite course. Whereas formerly their practice was insight-oriented and psychodynamic, over the years its focus has become more active and directive. The organized introduction of transactional analysis (TA) in 1983 is one factor contributing to this shift. Training programs were held with trainers from western Australia, after which a group of counselors and social workers embarked on a certification program. In 1989 they formed the Transactional Analysis Association of Singapore. The other active form of counseling in Singapore, family therapy, was contributed by the family- oriented counseling promoted by the Counseling and Care Centre. The center started to promote counseling that incorporated family therapy thinking and strategies in 1985, culminating in the launching of a postgraduate training program in 1990.

Yet another noticeable development in Singapore is the practice of reality therapy, particularly by the Pastoral Care and Guidance Unit of the Ministry of Education. The unit incorporated reality therapy and behavior modification in its work with students with behavioral problems.

As these developments show, then, counseling and therapy has indeed taken a more active form. More recently, active therapies such as strategic therapy, brief therapy, and solution-focused therapy were introduced, resulting in the four-step problem-solving approach known by the acronym PADI. (Yeo, 1992). This approach is reflected in the Counselor Training Program of the Counseling and Care Centre. Such a development has even led some counselors to explore the possibility of practicing single-session therapy as propounded by Moshe Talmon (1991).

The Training of Counselors.   The third aspect of development has to do with training. Currently no tertiary institution in Singapore offers a degree program in counseling. The National University of Singapore has a program leading to degrees in social work and psychology, whereas the National Institute of Education offers a program in pastoral care and guidance. In addition, most theological colleges include courses in counseling, and there is greater awareness of the need to increase the number of courses for theological students.

In 1981, in response to needs from workers in the helping profession, such as social workers, welfare workers, student and educational counselors, and doctors, the Counsellor Training Program (CTP) was launched. This nine-month part-time program provides training in counseling skills and sets the stage for further programs developed by the Counseling and Care Centre. The CTP started with a rather strong academic orientation, with emphasis on imparting knowledge in counseling. This program was reviewed, with assistance from Professor Myer Katz from McGill University in Montreal, Canada, in 1983. Katz was engaged as a consultant to the Counseling and Care Centre, and through his recommendation, training assumed a more practice-oriented focus.

Theoretical knowledge was reduced to a third of the program, with a great deal of emphasis on skill training, incorporating micro-skill training (Ivey, 1983) and the use of direct or live supervision. This form of supervision requires each trainee to work with clients behind a one-way mirror, observed by the rest of the training group and supervised by the trainer. Direct feedback is given via the telephone, and the trainee is also asked to leave the counseling room for consultation with the group before terminating each session. The use of video recording helps trainees to analyze their counseling sessions and gives them an opportunity to review their work. Together with small-group experience, trainees receive fairly intensive training in counseling.

The other program of the Counseling Centre is the Pastoral Training Program (PCP) which was launched in 1990 to enable pastors and church-related workers to acquire counseling skills for their work. This program is basically similar to the CTP except for reduced instruction in theories of counseling and inclusion of theological instruction related to counseling issues.

The most recent program is the diploma in family and marital therapy conducted in conjunction with the Institute of Family Therapy in London. Launched in 1991, this is a postgraduate program for mental health professionals designed to equip them with advanced knowledge and skills in working with clients from a family systems perspective. The primary teaching is done by trainers from the Counseling Centre with trainers from the institute who come sporadically during the program's two-year period. In order to graduate, trainees must fulfill the requirements of supervised clinical work with clients, present a dissertation, and submit videotapes of their clinical work for examination. All these programs offered by the Counseling Centre are part-time and are designed for those who are already involved in counseling. There are also short-term internship programs for those who wish to obtain concentrated practical training for one to three months. Other short-term programs have been developed from time to time.

Those who wish to pursue their degree programs in counseling must go abroad—for example, Malaysia and the Philippines, both of which have developed these programs.

Programs in counseling training are still inadequate in Singapore and have not kept pace with those in other disciplines. Psychological training is still academically oriented, though the future for the field of applied psychology holds much hope.

DIMENSIONS FOR THE FUTURE

The field of counseling in Singapore has a lot of room for growth. Counseling will continue to gain acceptance and professionalism will be enhanced, with increasing pressure to identify itself as a specialization. This outcome is in part a natural concomitant of the growing sophistication of an urbanized, technological society, populated by a middle-class society. As the profession grows, its emphasis will need to change to become relevant to a Singaporean society. This challenge is one for all professionals, whether they be practitioners or educators. Counseling practice will need to consider family focus, a consolidated approach, respect for hierarchy, normalizing abnormal behavior, and an integrative focus.

Family Focus

The individual-oriented focus of counseling must be viewed in relation to the family-oriented focus, for the individual's problem must always be examined within the context of the family. The aim should be family rather than individual development. When we help to deal with family relationships, the individual's problem is either reduced or made redundant altogether. Furthermore, his or her relationship would be improved, thus engaging the family as his or her primary support network. In any case, change in the individual will not be initiated without considering the effects on other family members.

Consolidated Approach

Although it is helpful to be familiar with all kinds of approaches in counseling, counselors must demonstrate competency in their practice. This competency can be achieved by being familiar with one approach that counselors can practice with a high level of proficiency. It augurs well for the profession if counselors can demonstrate specialized skills and be more concrete about what they can offer to deal with the client's problems.

Advocating a consolidated approach does not exclude the incorporation of other approaches and techniques. On the contrary, when counselors are clear about their basic skills, they can more easily incorporate other skills.

Respect for Hierarchy

While family relationships are becoming more democratic, many parents still find it rather offensive for children to talk directly to them. The father's position should be maintained, and proper respect should be accorded to him during the session. When grandparents are involved, they should be consulted on issues discussed. It is often unwise to encourage open, free-flowing communication between parents and children if parents are being

put in a vulnerable position. The counselor may have to separate
them and speak to the children and parents separately.

Normalizing Abnormal Behavior

When Singapore was less individualized, families found it easier
to accept or tolerate any erratic behavior from family members.
Now that people are busier, with family life undergoing change,
abnormal behavior is less tolerable. It would help to normalize
behavior and to avoid a strong medical, pathological view of
behavior. In this way we can bear with such behavior and maintain
the strength of the family. We should view problematic behavior
as ways to cope with difficult situations in life.

Integrative Focus

Counseling cannot ignore the totality of being human and should
accordingly focus on feelings, thinking, behavior, and the spiritual
life. The individual's spiritual aspect is important, for Singaporeans, like all other Asians, are very sensitive to the spiritual
forces that affect daily life.

ACTIONS FOR PROFESSIONAL DEVELOPMENT

Mental health professionals need to reexamine their approach
to their profession and develop more relevant models for the
Singaporean. Unfortunately, many professionals are not in direct
counseling roles. It is sometimes a secondary or minor role that
does not help with effective development of models. Furthermore,
most, if not all, of those who teach counseling are nonpractitioners.
Frequently, they do not have sufficient interaction and dialogue
with practitioners. To this end those who teach counseling should
maintain a practice base and engage in dialogue with practitioners.
In addition, training centers like the Counseling and Care Centre
should maintain a level of competency that promotes the counsel-

ing profession. There is also a need to develop local materials and to produce publications that reflect the integration of Western models with local context. Better still, publications on an indigenized counseling practice are needed.

Professional counselors should make time for reflection and integration so that they can do the work of contextualization. Meeting together to consolidate their position is of equal value. Thus, rather than import new ideas or approaches, they should reflect on current practices and develop local models within the Singaporean context.

Finally, counselors should be trained by Singaporeans with resources from Asia rather than the West. This is not to suggest that non-Asian professionals should be excluded, but that a balance between the two should be maintained to ensure that Asian interests receive priority.

CONCLUSION

At this time Singapore should take stock of developments in counseling. The profession has developed to the point where counselors should make careful assessments of where they are going. The future holds great promise for counseling from a distinctively Singaporean perspective.

REFERENCES

Counseling and Care Centre. (1982). *Annual Reports*, 1971, 1982. Singapore.

Counseling and Care Centre. (1991). 25th Anniversary Publication, 1991. Singapore.

Ivey, A. (1983). *Intentional Interviewing and Counseling*. Monterey, Calif.: Brooks/Cole Publishing Co.

Samaritans of Singapore. (1982, 1992). *Annual Reports*. Singapore.

Singapore Association for Counseling. *Constitution*.

The Sunday Times. (May 3, 1992). Singapore.

Talman, M. (1991). *Single Session Therapy*. San Francisco: Jossey-Bass Publishers.

Yeo, A. *Counseling: A Problem-Solving Approach*. (In process)

Yeo, A. (1990). Developments and trends of counseling in Singapore—a personal view. *Asian Bulletin of Counseling* 1 (1).

3. Guidance and Counseling in Indonesia

J. T. LOBBY LOEKMONO

Despite the broad scope suggested by the title of this chapter, here we deal only with the historical development of guidance and counseling, the professionalization of workers in guidance and counseling, and the challenges facing counseling in the 1990s.

A HISTORICAL PERSPECTIVE

Guidance and counseling in Indonesia had its beginnings in the realm of formal education, namely, the schools. In contrast, in the United States guidance and counseling originated within the community. In fact, in Indonesia the discipline existed long before the war of Indonesian independence, which was finally gained on August 17, 1945. When Indonesia was under Dutch control, the main aim of education was to prepare the people for colonial service. On May 20, 1908 a movement known as Boedi Oetomo (the Essential Character) began with the overall goal of developing the nation in all areas of culture. This movement influenced educational thinkers to become nationalistically oriented. Among them were Ki Hajar Dewantara (1922), who founded the Perguruan Nasional Taman Siswa (National Educational Students Park), R. A. Kartini, the national heroine who founded the Kartini Women's School in Java, and Mohamad Safei (1926), whose occupational school in Sumatra devoted a great deal of attention to students' vocational needs. Thus, guidance and counseling can be said to have been in existence since 1908, while Frank Parson was founding his Vocational Bureau in Boston.

Regrettably, guidance and counseling in the field of education was not able to develop inasmuch as the Republic of Indonesia was still being colonized. Moreover, the education system at the time gave little support to guidance and counseling. M. Surya (1988), in his book *Dasar-Dasar Konseling Pendidikan* (Introduction to Educational Counseling) divided the development of guidance and counseling in Indonesia into six decades.

The first decade, the Decade Before the War of Independence, occurred prior to the 1940s. During this time attention was given to efforts to gain Indonesia's independence through education. This movement, founded by Ki Hajar Dewantara and his National Educational Students Park, took as its motto: "Ing ngarso sung tulada, ing madyo mangun karso, tut wuri handayani" [Those in front show an example, those in the middle show their will, and those at the back keep pace]. This motto initiated and became the basis of educational practice as well as guidance as a whole in Indonesia.

The second decade, the 1940s, was the so-called Decade of Struggle. This period represents an important watershed in the history of Indonesia: namely, its recognition as a free country on August 17, 1945. Ki Hajar Dewantara became the first minister of education and culture in the Republic of Indonesia. Guidance had still not gained much attention because Indonesia was facing problems of backwardness and underdevelopment. There was also the question of how the new Republic of Indonesia could make the people understand themselves as free citizens of a free country. Understanding oneself is a primary focus of guidance and counseling.

The third decade was the 1950s, the Decade of Challenge. After independence, the new republic was still unstable, with considerable unrest and coups developing aimed at destabilizing the nation from both within and without. The problems of backwardness, illiteracy, and underdevelopment continued to challenge the field of education. In 1950 the Basic Laws pertaining to education were successfully formulated. Guidance and counseling was implicitly included in the various educational activities.

In the fourth decade, the 1960s, the Decade of Pioneering Effort, the fruits of pioneering efforts became apparent, including the encouragement by educational managers that schools should offer guidance and counseling, the offering of courses in guidance and counseling at teacher training colleges, and the offering of guidance and counseling modules therein to all students; the holding of workshops; the training of teachers or guidance workers in schools; and publications on guidance and counseling. However, yet another significant obstacle arose in Indonesia: namely, the communist coup in 1965, which hampered the development of education, including guidance and counseling.

In the fifth decade, the 1970s, the Decade of Structuring, an effort was made to structure and implement guidance in schools. In addition, the legal aspects, as well as the related concepts and the necessary implementations, were faced in an orderly manner. Support was offered to the development of the "Orde Baru" (the New Order), or the "order for development," which looked to development in all areas, including education. Educational developments were channeled into (1) equal opportunities for study; (2) quality; (3) relevancy; and (4) efficiency. Thus, the 1975 curriculum made guidance and counseling an integral component in the educational process. Consequently, *The Guidance and Counseling Curriculum Handbook for Schools* (Book III.C) was produced, and schools recruited teacher-counselors or counselors. Workshops were held at the area and national levels. In 1975 a professional guidance organization known as Ikatan Petugas Bimbingan Indonesia (the Indonesian Guidance Workers Association) was formed. A master's program in guidance and counseling at the teacher training college in Bandung, West Java, was introduced, and research and other activities took place in the area of guidance and counseling.

The sixth decade, the 1980s, the Decade of Stabilizing, is called stabilizing because an attempt was made to consolidate guidance both within and outside schools into a better service. Various activities took place during this decade:

1. Curriculum perfecting (1975), which gave rise to the 1984 curriculum requiring schools to carry out guidance and counseling, specifically career guidance.

2. The implementation of compulsory schooling for primary school-age children.

3. The successful formulation of the National Educational Legal System (1989) elaborated in government regulations Nos. 27, 28, 29, and 30, which replaced the laws on education set down in 1950. These government regulations further established guidance and counseling as a service to be provided at all levels and in all forms of education.

4. The letter of authority No. 26/1989 from the National Minister for National Resource Utilization, which gave the credits due to teachers, including teacher-counselors, under the ambit of the Republic of Indonesia's Department of Education and Culture.

5. In the field of education, the development of careful structure and implementation of guidance and counseling. Because of the emphasis on development, career guidance was made a priority beginning in 1984.

6. The update of the curriculum for those studying guidance and counseling in teacher training colleges. Training became based on competency in order to realize the aim of producing professionally competent counselors.

7. The cooperation of the Indonesian Guidance Workers Association (IPBI) with the government and other groups of professionals such as psychologists and teachers at both the national and international level, such as with Asian Regional Association for Vocational and Educational Guidance (ARAVEG), Association of Psychological and Educational Counselors of Asia (APECA), and American Association for Counseling and Development (AACD).

8. The conduct of workshops, seminars, and training sessions at both the area and national level, as well as within Asia, for teacher-counselors and counselors by the Department of Education and Culture and by other professional organizations such as IPBI.

According to Andi Mapiare in his book *Pengantar Bimbingan dan Konseling di Sekolah* (Introduction to Guidance and Counseling in Schools, 1984), the development of guidance and counseling in Indonesia can be divided into four periods, namely: the Seed (1922–1960); the Growth of Educational Guidance (1960–1971); the Renewal of Educational Guidance (1971–1983); and the Modern/Professionalization of Educational Guidance (1983–). Based on the author's informal observation, guidance and counseling in Indonesia in the 1990s faces the challenge of professionalism. This concern was projected by the author at the eighth APECA conference in Penang, Malaysia, as the Indonesian Country Report.

PROFESSIONALIZATION OF GUIDANCE AND COUNSELING WORKERS

Prerequisites and Nature of the Profession

Why should it be necessary to discuss the professionalization of workers in guidance and counseling in education? Isn't guidance and counseling a profession? These are two of the pressing questions that may come to mind at this point. In his book *Professional Counseling* (1981), F. A. Nugent proposed five requirements or inherent qualities of a profession, which all its members should uphold, namely, ability to clearly define its role; ability to offer specialized, unique service, special knowledge, and skills; a code of ethics relating to the work of counselors; the right to perform and carry out services; the competency to practice professionally. Consequently, as summarized by Prayitno (1987), Nugent states that, before it can be considered truly professional, the field of counseling services must be prepared to move forward and succeed at six developmental tasks:

1. Social service, which is unique and carried out by counselors, must be so conceived as to be clearly separate from that which is carried out by others or other experts.

2. Standards in areas of selection and training of trainee counselors must be developed. Such standards should be agreed upon by other professional groups and by those institutions that offer counseling services.

3. An accreditation procedure must be set up for institutions that offer counseling services, in order to ensure that such standards are both useful and on target.

4. For the certification to be truly valid, counselors produced by these institutions should attain (at the very least) a minimum standard of competency.

5. Counselors who already possess professional counseling qualifications should actively promote their professional development and autonomy, so as to enable them to carry out their unique service. Counselors as a group must also be ready to take on the work of counseling.

6. Counselors as a group must hold and apply a code of ethics that will govern and control the behavior of group members. Based on observations arrived at by attendance of the National Guidance Conventions and Congresses of Indonesian Guidance Workers Association (Ikatan Petugas Bimbingan Indonesia = IPBI) from 1975 until March 1989 in Denpasar, Bali, IPBI and its members have already fulfilled four of the professional requirements laid down by Nugent (1981). Progress is still very much needed in the last two requirements: namely, the right to perform their role and carry out their services as conceived, and competency in practicing professionally. IPBI must continue to seek and apply standards as conceived and come to possess the necessary skills for monitoring and carrying out the developmental tasks in the future, especially 4, 5, and 6 above as discussed by McCully.

In order to meet these challenges or to solve these problems in the context of professionalism in guidance and counseling in Indonesia, four alternative answers, or strategies, can be postulated:

1. Avoid the issue. This alternative seemingly solves the problem successfully, that is, by not having to face the problem itself. All are content for the moment, but the future may bring fatal consequences as professionalism becomes even more remote for guidance workers. While those in other professions mock the professionalism of guidance and counseling, even the community with qualified staff may not come to trust it as a profession.

2. Solve the problem with enforced regulation. The IPBI, for example, could use its influence and resources to affect the decision-making process. Thereby it could come to be legally recognized as a professional organization, and its members subsequently could be recognized as professional guidance workers. This strategy might appear to offer the best shortcut, but the result will not last.

3. Accommodate to the contextual conditions and situation as they are. Thus, guidance and counseling workers would simply adjust themselves to the demands made on them by parties that happened to possess the authority. A strategy that might be adopted here would be for counselors to form groups and become members of the Indonesian Psychology Graduates Association. Psychologists are better known in the community than either guidance workers or counselors; thus, counselors might then continue to offer their services, which are in fact psychological in nature. Could this strategy help foster the professionalism of workers of guidance and counseling? A counselor could be part of a profession at the same level as a psychologist, a psychiatrist, and a doctor.

4. Strive toward the professionalism of guidance and counseling workers. This strategy is the most appropriate choice for us, for three reasons: First, there is inconsistency in the professional standards of guidance and counseling workers with students in education; second, the competence of student guidance and counseling workers in education is not yet clearly recognized; and, third, there is a disparity among student guidance and counseling workers in education.

Under these alternatives, guidance and counseling would develop to the point where an independent profession would emerge, separate from and yet with the same status as other professions.

THE ROLE OF GUIDANCE AND COUNSELING IN EDUCATION

Guidance and counseling in elementary and junior high schools in Indonesia as stated in the 1975 curriculum forms one of the integral components of the total educational process carried out in schools, along with maintaining a proper curriculum and an efficient educational administration. In the 1984 curriculum upgrading, guidance and counseling was proposed as one of three activities of equal importance to schools, namely: development of knowledge, attitudes and values, skills, and creativity through studies conducted efficiently and effectively; a sufficient school administrative process; and provision of special assistance in the form of guidance services for pupils to develop themselves.

These three activities form the essence of the program and may not be separated one from the other. What then is the role of guidance and counseling services in higher education? Their role may be evaluated from the aspects of the needs and problems faced by the students. An example, taken from the reports of the counseling service at Satya Wacana Christian University Counseling Centre, Salatiga, shows that between 1974 and 1984 family, relationship, and psychological problems were the most common problems of students coming for counseling service. Among the most common study problems were grade point average below 2.00, which results in a warning from the academic advisor; choice of the wrong course of studies; need to enter a course of studies that is in line with interests; a study system that does not cope with the demands created by the credit load; feelings of loneliness while in class; and problems in carrying out or completing a thesis.

The most frequent relationship problems brought up were problems of personal relationships; development of cliques in class;

Table 3.1
Responses to the Mooney Problem Checklist

Problem Category	Item Total	%
Adjustment to College work	7, 196	45.34
Social and recreational activities	6, 565	41.36
The future : Vocational and Educational	6, 093	38.39
Morals and Religion	5, 540	34.90
Social–Psychological Relations	5, 216	32.86
Personal–Psychological Relations	5, 114	32.22
Courtship, Sex, Marriages	5, 058	31.87
Curriculum and teaching Procedure	4, 839	30.49
Finance, Living Conditions and Employment	4, 679	29.48
Health and Physical Development	4, 048	25.73
Home and Family	3, 807	23.98

Note: The categorization of the seriousness of the problem, expressed in percentage terms, is as follows: 1–25% not serious, 25.01–50% fairly serious (needing counseling), 50.01–75% serious, 75.01–100% very serious.

Source: Loekmono et al. (1989).

broken boyfriend/girlfriend relationships; and unhappiness sharing accommodation with others. The psychological problems most often discussed with a counselor were feelings of inferiority and isolation; lack of self-acceptance; and perceptions of having a character deficit. The family problems brought up tended to be related to a deprived social-economic situation experienced by the family: one family member becoming ill; lack of harmony between parents; and parents demanding a high performance level beyond the ability of the child.

Research carried out on 529 students at Satya Wacana Christian University by Loekmono et al. (1988) in the academic year 1987–1988 presented the students' various problems as identified by the Mooney Problem Checklist. Results are presented in Table 3.1.

Based on the study of problems found among students and the types of problems they experienced, we can conclude that there is a significant negative correlation between the number of problems confronting students and their grade point average. This suggests that students need to reduce or to overcome their problems. Furthermore, it suggests that lecturers, academic advisors, and counselors in higher education should offer guidance and counseling to students.

WHO IS TO HELP STUDENTS?

Guidance and counseling services in junior high schools and in high schools possess a variety of guidance and counseling staff. Some guidance workers, for example, are taken from the teaching staff and have had no training in the field of guidance and counseling. Other guidance workers are teachers who have been able to obtain basic guidance and counseling training from a week to three months' duration. Yet others hold a three-year diploma in guidance and counseling and, despite coming from various backgrounds, have attended the relevant lectures over one year (two semesters). Some guidance workers graduate with a three-year diploma or have a first degree purely in guidance and counseling. And finally some guidance workers graduate from institutions with an honors degree in educational psychology and counseling, or in guidance and counseling teaching counseling. Those with master's degrees usually fill roles as consultants or coordinators of guidance and counseling in the junior high schools. The guidance workers in the junior high and high schools are mostly those who have a week to three months of basic training, or those who have joined a three-year diploma crash program. These groups operate in the field. Presently, the number of workers qualified in guidance and counseling, compared with other workers, is not very great.

With regard to higher education, the situation pertaining to guidance and counseling workers is not very different there than it is at the junior high schools or the high schools. The workers in higher education may be grouped together as follows:

1. Counselors who are lecturers but have neither knowledge nor training in guidance and counseling. These counselors may be senior staff members. It can be tragic when such lecturers are taken in as student guidance and counseling workers merely for want of meeting the quota of teaching hours.

2. Counselors who have been counseling lecturers, who have had the opportunity to obtain three months of basic training at the Universitas Indonesia-Jakarta, at the Universitas Pajajaran-Bandung, or at the Universitas Gajah Mada (Psychology Faculty)-Jogyakarta.

3. Counselors who are staff members of a teacher training faculty. There is a phasing out of such a stream.

4. Counselors with a background in guidance and counseling, such as those who graduated under the old degree system, or with honors, or holding master's or doctorate degrees in guidance and counseling.

The guidance and counseling workers in higher education are mostly from groups 1 and 2 above, with a few from group 4. This situation has occurred not because the counseling staff came out of institutions that taught counseling, but because of the unclear status of those who become student guidance and counseling workers. It is still the case of graduates from an institution who taught counseling and yet preferred to become regular course lecturers because they would be classified as educational staff and not as administrative staff. The career ladder is easily negotiated if one becomes a lecturer rather than a student guidance and counseling worker. As a result of this factor, many positions as student guidance and counseling workers are filled by counselors who are only doing guidance part-time. Is guidance and counseling not a professional task? Why is this professional service not given full attention? This task requires professional handling. Thus, this whole situation makes us realize that it is a question not just of bringing in staff, but of recruiting special staff who have been trained by institutions teaching counseling and who have the relevant competencies acceptable to those in higher education. Hence, the quality of counseling offered and the function and character of counselors must be in line with that expected of student guidance and counseling workers in higher education.

At Satya Wacana all the counselors come from an honors degree background in guidance and counseling or are given the opportunity to progress to the master's level. In carrying out their work as counselors serving in the counseling center, they work with psychologists and doctors on the campus, as well as with pastoral psychiatrists. The various professions involved in giving this aid must be able to work together in helping students with problems. Student problems must be approached in an holistic way, for no problem stands alone; rather there are various interrelated aspects. We have moved from opposing fragmentary services getting their own way, but we should also start to consider the best way in which these various professions can work together in order to help individuals with particular needs or problems.

Various units exist in higher education to help students—for example, assistant rectors, deans, academic advisors, guidance and counseling staff, health center staff, student chaplains, friends, student organizations, the librarian, student hostel leaders, and so forth. Research at Satya Wacana Christian University in 1982 showed the following:

1. Students with health problems choose the health center.
2. Students with psychological problems choose the counseling center.
3. Students with problems in planning their studies choose their academic advisor.
4. Students with problems of job seeking choose the counseling center.
5. Students with spiritual problems choose the student chaplains and the counseling center.
6. Students with study problems choose the counseling center and their academic advisor.
7. Students with adjustment or friendship problems choose the counseling center or their academic advisor.
8. Students with financial problems choose the assistant rector for financial affairs, or their friends.
9. Students with accommodation problems choose a student friend or the counseling center.

10. Students with sexual problems choose a student friend or the counseling center.

11. Students with problems in their family choose the counseling center or a friend.

The counseling center helps with virtually all categories of problems, with the exception of health and financial problems and problems in planning studies. Other students also become sources of refuge for students experiencing problems. What then is the role of the counseling center and of workers in guidance and counseling with students in general? How do we equip ourselves with the necessary knowledge and skills to be able to help such students? How can we help students who are being contacted by their friends experiencing problems? One answer to these questions is to hold training sessions for those students interested in helping their friends, through peer counseling. We should admit that the guidance and counseling workers in higher education cannot work alone, and if the service offered is to be successful, counselors must be willing to work with all the staff members in higher education, as well as with those outside the realm of higher education.

Even though this is evidently true, the professionalism of guidance and counseling workers remains the best strategy, because students have a right to obtain professional help from such workers. Guidance and counseling focuses on attending to the needs of the counselees and other clients. Thus, broadly speaking the counselor's role or function is to carry out activities such as individual counseling, guidance and counseling in groups, and academic guidance through the planning of studies and the choice of courses, career guidance and counseling, measurement, assessment and testing, consultation, coordination as regards making referral relationships, community relations, and professional development.

With the handing down of the letter of authority from the national minister for National Resource Utilization No. 26/Menpan/1989, many subject heads and head teachers were willing to become teacher-counselors. Consequently, there would be a teacher-counselor for every 150 students.

CRITICISM AND CHALLENGE

Students' criticisms and discontent with workers in charge of the student guidance and counseling include the following:

1. Workers in charge of student guidance and counseling do not offer adequate help to the students. They are merely concerned with clerical jobs in the office and are nowhere to be seen when needed.

2. They are more concerned with students who have specific problems than with the majority of students who are not having problems but still need guidance and development.

3. More time is spent on personal counseling rather than on consultation or on an approach with a wider scope. (In the universities, as well as in the junior and high schools, the counselor's counseling skills and techniques are not well developed.)

4. There is little interaction between workers in charge of guidance and counseling with other professions, but they depend a lot on other professions.

5. Workers in charge of the Guidance and Counseling Unit don't keep up with new scientific developments; as a result, they do not improve.

6. The counselor in universities focuses more on therapy than on career guidance or placement services. Graduates from Indonesian universities find it increasingly difficult to find a job.

7. Not many workers in charge of the Guidance and Counseling Unit know about the world of work and are not sufficiently able to assist students with solving job or career problems.

8. Workers in the Guidance and Counseling Unit act authoritatively and tend to give much advice.

These criticisms should help guidance and counseling workers, especially those in the school setting, to develop their professionalism. Guidance and counseling services, which include various aspects of life, will enable the students to prepare themselves for adulthood and to become members of a community and qualified citizens (independent, self-constructive, and community-constructive). With Indonesia's present goal of national development, and its theme of participation, elevating the individual's standing in particular and Indonesian people in general, guidance and counseling students who participate will find it a challenge. The task of counselors will be harder in the future. However, their preparation will be even more exciting. Inadequate preparation could lead to stress. Unity, perseverance, and professional vitality are required to upgrade workers in charge of student guidance and counseling and cooperation with professional organizations like APECA and ARAVEG.

Four main components define the counselor's professionalism. First, a professional organization like IPBI has the following division: Organization of Indonesian Guidance Graduates or Organization of Indonesian Counselors. By attending science meetings, the counselors can improve their knowledge, skill, and personality. A professional organization like IPBI also serves as a caretaker to make sure that the counselor acts in accordance with the ethical codes of counseling.

Second, counselors who are doing fieldwork are expected to show a high standard of dedication to their profession. A worker in charge of the Guidance and Counseling Unit in the university is not clear about his or her career ladder stage when entering the unit. He or she belongs to the administrative force. It would be easier to join the academic force where the career ladder stage is well defined and attainable. This condition is different with workers in the junior or high schools because the workers there are called teacher-counselors. This is one reason why student guidance and counseling in the universities has become stagnant. Hence, the profession of counseling is not likely to develop because the counselors themselves do not show much interest. On the other hand, a contradictory stream might arise in which the guidance and counseling graduates have prepared themselves well for the student Guidance and Counseling Unit.

In either case, the problem of support and management should be handled positively, and a way out should be provided. As a private university, Satya Wacana has to consider whether a counselor in the counseling center belongs to the academic force, to administration, research, social welfare, the library, or the academic staff. (For example, a counselor counseling seventeen students for an hour is evaluated at one credit. A counselor should carry out a workload of twelve credits every semester, with emphasis on developing the student's dedication to the community and teaching. Research and administration are equal to zero credits.) Such a solution should be worked out. If the counselors doing fieldwork are able to develop themselves better, the counseling profession will gradually be better appreciated.

Third, the institute of counselor education decides the counselors' professionalism. Specifically, it decides whether the profession of counseling is popular within the community. What is needed is counselor quality, not quantity. The institute should focus not only on the school setting but on the setting outside the school as well. In an important breakthrough, Satya Wacana has initiated nondegree programs like industrial counseling (four semesters) and social counseling (six semesters) in an effort to expand the profession's potential.

The fourth component, students who are potential counselors, is critical because they will be the succeeding generation striving to professionalize guidance and counseling in the future. Hard work and good performance are required from those who are still taking courses. They are challenged to become competent counselors and dedicated to their profession. The master's and doctoral degrees have been added in the teacher training college (Bandung, Malang, or Jakarta).

Integrating these four components into one system will enhance the professionalism of Indonesia's guidance and counseling services.

THE CHALLENGES OF THE 1990s

Based on the author's informal observations as a counselor of students at Satya Wacana in the 1980s, counselees can be characterized as follows:

Counselees appear for help only when their problems are severe, even though they may have decided to contact a counselor some months before. They initially hold unrealistic expectations as to the help they may receive from their counselors, and they are dependent. Conversational informalities in the process of counseling take up a relatively large amount of time; only then will the counselees share their problem. (There is the feeling that circumlocutions allow them to sound out the possibility of becoming open.) Counselees tend to come only once or twice, except for those with clinical problems who are scheduled to appear regularly.

There is no general understanding as to what constitutes consultation, a counseling interview, or counseling. Generally, a taboo is still attached to discussions of sexual matters or politics; however, counselees who are students are beginning to be more open on these issues. Finally, in choosing their counselors, most counselees will take into account seniority and professional background.

Indonesia is said to have 179,321,641 inhabitants on thousands of islands, giving it the fifth position in the world population ranking. The island of Java has 65 percent of the total population, making it the most densely populated island in the world. Indonesia is also rich in language, tradition, and religions, adding to the challenge and interest of counseling. Apart from the rich environment, numerous potential constraints challenge the guidance workers. Living under the motto "Bhineka Tunggal Ika" (unity in diversity) means that every citizen or individual who comes under it must be well adjusted, exhibiting a tolerant approach but not losing their individuality.

A number of challenges lie ahead. In the future, counseling must be effective and efficient because economic considerations dominate the interests of counselees or individuals in general (Naisbitt and Aburdene, 1990). Counseling for peacetime conditions needs to be developed now that the global economic boom produced a widespread reluctance to engage in warfare, and attention is diverted to leisure activities and environmental causes (Naisbitt and Aburdene, 1990). Cooperation with extracurricular teachers, especially those in arts and crafts, is needed in order to guide and to follow up the process of counseling given by counselors to students (Naisbitt and Aburdene, 1990).

A global lifestyle and cultural nationalism challenge the counselor to become skilled in the management of conflict, for the two are in opposition. A global lifestyle needs to be emulated and the positive values of traditional culture have to be developed. How can Indonesian values find their place in the process of counseling? What counseling approaches are appropriate for Indonesian culture? Rogerian, rational-emotive, Gestalt, cognitive, reality, and so forth? (Naisbitt and Aburdene, 1990).

One of the main objectives of counseling in the future is to assist individuals in the optimal development of human resources and to help individuals achieve independence (Naisbitt and Aburdene, 1990). The ethical and moral awareness of counselors is under challenge in this technological and information age.

A value shift has taken place among the youth, as a result of which the younger generation does not yet hold a settled, organized view of life. Thus, they are all too easily influenced by negative tendencies such as smoking, drugs, and promiscuity, without showing any awareness of wrongdoing, or regret. The confusion that has resulted from the rapid rate of change has caused personal relationships to become an area of difficulty in the modern era, thus causing dissension among students. These circumstances may well underlie the rise of the biological century, particularly as regards genetic engineering. What counseling approach, for example, should be used for a child who is a test-tube baby? Or with life expectancy increasing, leading to a growing number of elderly, how are counselors to work in the new field of counseling the aged (Naisbitt and Aburdene, 1990).

One result of modernization has been the development of religion as an academic area of knowledge; technology has been found to be unable to answer questions on the meaning of life. Here the challenge for counselors is to provide a spiritual, pastoral counseling service for adults.

Individual counseling will continue to increase with the increasing prosperity of individuals. With the development of the hukum karma doctrine (the Javanese philosophy of cause and effect, whereby one's fate is determined by one's deeds), individual counseling and group counseling must develop a new shade. Group counseling must come to be based on the individual who is valued, given space, counted on to participate, and perform as a group member—all these will become important considerations in time to come.

All these challenges lead to the problem of identifying the counselors and guidance workers or guidance teachers in schools. Who is to be known as the guidance teacher in a school? The head teacher? A subject head who is also responsible for guidance? A class teacher? A trainee teacher? A graduate from a guidance and counseling course or anyone with a course in educational psychology and guidance?

CONCLUSION

The great variety of workers who are in charge of student guidance and counseling or the counseling center is an asset rather than a liability when the job designation is clear. The success of student guidance and counseling services depends on team integration and cooperation. Standards of counselor professionalism in student guidance and counseling in schools should define the minimum competency for graduates and for those who have followed the master's and doctoral programs. In the field of guidance and counseling in Indonesia, a great deal of homework remains to be done in the area of guidance and counseling as Indonesia approaches the year 2000 and the third millennium. Challenges can be uplifting, and at the same time they can destroy enthusiasm. Hopefully, the counselor's personality is well adjusted, so that in time these challenges will be experienced as elevating. Truly, it can be said that without challenges the profession of counseling is like food without spice.

REFERENCES

Aubrey, F. (1982). A house divided: guidance and counseling in 20th-century. *Personnel and Guidance Journal*, 61–64, 198–204.

Beek, M. V. (1987). *Konseling Pastoral* [Pastoral counseling]. Semarang, Indonesia: Satya Wacana.

Daldjoeni, N. (1990). Pergantian Abad Yang Meresahkan Dalam Tumbuh dan Berkembang. [Replacing a century of anxiety in growth and development] (edisi khusus) Salatiga, *Majalah Kritis Universitas Kristen Satya Wacana*.

Departemen Pendidikan dan Kebudayaan RI. (1976). *Kurikulum Pedoman Bimbingan dan Penyuluhan di Sekolah* [Curriculum guide to school guidance and counseling]. Buku III.C, Jakarta: Balai Pustaka.

Ibrahim, A., Helms, J., and Thompson, Donald L. (1983). Counselor role and function: an approach by consumer and counselor. *Personnel and Guidance Journal*, 61–64, 597–601.

Loekmono, L., et al. (1988). *Saling Menolong Antar Mahasiswa* [Helping between undergraduates]. Semarang: Percetakan Satya Wacana.

Mapiare, A. (1984). *Pengantar Bimbingan dan Konseling di Sekolah* [An introduction of guidance and counseling in schools]. Surabaya, Indonesia: Penerbit Usaha Nasional.

Naisbitt, J., and Aburdene, P. (1990). *Megatrends 2000* (FX Budiyanto, trans.). Jakarta, Indonesia: Binapura Aksara.

Nugent, F. A. (1981). *Professional Counseling*. Monterey, Calif.: Brooks/Cole Publications.

Othman, A. H., and Awang, A. (1990 May). Counseling in Asia: Challenges and Strategies for the 1990's. Paper presented at 8th APECA Biennial Conference Workshop, Pulau Pinang, Malaysia.

Prayitno. (1987). *Professionalisasi Konseling dan Pendidikan Konselor* [Professionalization of counseling and counselor education]. Jakarta: Dirjen Dikti Proyek Pengembangan Lembaga Pendidikan Tenaga Kependidikan.

Report. (1975). *Konvensi Nasional Bimbingan dan Kongres I IPBI* [National guidance convention and congress]. Malang.

Report. (1976). *Konvensi Nasional Bimbingan II dan Simposium Bimbingan Jabatan II, IPBI* [National guidance convention and guidance symposium]. Salatiga: IPBI.

Report. (1982). *Penelitian Mahasiswa: Batak, Cina, Dayak, Jawa dan Sumba di UKSW* [Undergraduate study: Batak, Chinese, Dayak, Javanese and Sumba at UKSW]. Salatiga: Pusat Bimbingan.

Report. (1988). *Penelitian Korelasi Masalah Mahasiswa dan Indeks Prestasi Kumulatif Semester I Tahun Akademik 1987/1988 Mahasiswa UKSW* [A study of the relationship of undergraduate problems and the indices of cumulative achievement]. Salatiga: Pusat Bimbingan Universitas Kristen Satya Wacana.

Report. (1989). *Konvensi Nasional Bimbingan VII dan Kongres VI, Ikatan Petugas Bimbingan Indonesia* [National guidance convention and congress]. Denpasar—Bali.

Soewondo, S., and Markam, S. (1985). *Sistem Pelayanan Bimbingan dan Konseling di Perguruan Tinggi* [Guidance and counseling system in higher education]. Jakarta: Direktorat Jendral Pendidikan Tinggi RI.

Surya, M. (1988). *Dasar-Dasar Konseling Pendidikan (Teori & Concept)* [Introduction to educational counseling—theory and concept]. Yogyakarta: Kota Kembang.

Wilson, H., and Rotter, C. (1982). School counseling: a look into the future. *Personnel and Guidance Journal*, 60–66, 353–357.

4. Counseling and Mental Health Among the Chinese

HERBERT CHIU

A culture delineates for its people a unique orientation toward life, norms for interpersonal behavior, and ways of understanding themselves, the world, the universe, and their positions in them. Explicit or not, people within a culture understand in their own terms what is worth striving for. They have their unique version of what an ideal life is like and therefore an ideal personality, an ideal family, an ideal group, an ideal community, and an ideal country. Because socialization into a culture begins early in life, people tend to see their ways of life as necessary and relevant but seldom have the opportunity to think of it otherwise—until they open up themselves to new ways. As Eisenberg (1981) writes:

> we are equally blind to the effects of the "cultural field" (akin to the gravitational field) on biobehavioural phenomena because we think and act within a cultural "coordinate system." We only become aware of the field forces of our cultural system when we extend our vision to the study of other times, other places and other modes of social organization (p. 35).

Since mental health is a social psychological phenomenon that has close ties with concepts relating to ideal personality and ways of life, it is important to identify the characteristics of Chinese culture, with special reference to ideal personality and ways of life in order to be an effective counselor.

CHARACTERISTICS OF THE
CHINESE MIND—COLLECTIVISM

Historians and anthropologists have their own unique ways of identifying the characteristics of the Chinese mind. Turning to the Chinese classics that explicate their philosophy and their ideals of life may mislead the empiricist, for the Chinese classics are the properties of the learned. People in all walks of life in Chinese societies may present different pictures that may be based on dominant moral and religious thoughts or doctrines, such as vulgar Confucianism, Daoism, and Buddhism, which could be very different from the Chinese classics (Chiu, 1990).

Empirical studies conducted by cross-cultural researchers show a number of cross-disciplinary consistencies. For example, Hofstede's work-related value survey (1980; 1983) factors out four dimensions: individualism, masculinity, power distance, and uncertainty avoidance out of fifty-three cultural units. Cultures are then compared by means of their relative locations circumscribed by the dimensions. Hong Kong, Taiwan, and Singapore all scored high on the collectivism end of the individualism-collectivism scale and moderately high in power distance. According to Hofstede (1983):

> Collectivism stands for a preference for a tightly knit social framework in which individuals can expect their relatives, clan, or other in-group to look after them in exchange for unquestioning loyalty. ... The fundamental issue addressed by this dimension is the degree of interdependence a society maintains among individuals. It relates to people's self-concept: "I" or "we."
>
> Power distance is the extent to which the members of a society accept that power institutions and organizations are distributed unequally. This affects the behaviour of the less powerful as well

as of the more powerful members of society. People in large power distance societies accept a hierarchical order in which everybody has a place that needs no further justification. People in small power distance societies strive for power equalization and demand justification for power inequalities. The fundamental issue addressed by this dimension is how a society handles inequalities among people when they occur (p. 340).

To develop a measure of values that reflects the indigenous themes and concerns of Chinese culture, the Chinese culture connection study (1987), by means of ecological factor analysis of one hundred thousand employees in forty countries, identified "Confucian work dynamism" as a factor representative of Hong Kong and Taiwan employees. Both aspects of the Confucian ethic are outlined as follows—the creation of dedicated, motivated, responsible, and educated individuals and the enhanced sense of commitment, organizational identity, and loyalty to various institutions (Kahn, 1979). Empirical researchers have described a distinct way of life (ethics) represented by Confucianism that is applicable even to the Chinese who live outside China.

Items on the integration and moral discipline of the Chinese culture connection study and on power distance and individualism clustered together in a second-order factor analysis represented by collectivism. Sizable correlations were found between "human heartedness" and Hofstede's "masculinity-femininity." Common to these dimensions is the opposition between human-centered and task-centered considerations informing collective activities.

CHINESE PERSONALITY TRAITS

The characteristic traits of the Chinese people have been vividly described by Cheng (1946). One characteristic trait, patience, manifested itself in the form of racial, religious, political, and deprivation tolerance. According to Cheng, the Chinese people repressed desires or impulses that were unacceptable in their society. They were the greatest fatalists in the world and were preeminently frugal. Moreover, they considered humility to be a great virtue. The Chinese were generally quite contented with whatever little they had and were extremely conservative. They were a peaceful people, and they believed that in conflicts of any kind justice and reason always prevailed in the long run. They were not particular about accuracy and precision.

These characteristic traits were confirmed not only through large-scale cross-cultural studies but also micro studies at the individual level by means of the Rorschach test as done at an early date by Abel and Hsu (1949). They discovered that:

> The Chinese for centuries have worked out a way of life where the external role of the individual becomes adjusted to the pattern dictated by Chinese society. By following this "status personality," it would be expected that all individual differences would not be ironed out and that different individuals would find it more or less hard to conform to a status personality rather than attempting to work out for themselves modes of behaving and feeling more idiosyncratic and more in keeping with their individual psychological make-up. In the Rorschach results we have seen something of how this Chinese status personality functions by conformity and control (p. 300).

Here, again we see the influence of collectivism and power distance on the personality of Chinese people. According to Hui and Villareal (1989), the correlational patterns portray collectivists in both the United States and Hong Kong as being high in need for affiliation, nurturance, and succorance, and low in need for autonomy.

The Importance of "Face"

The desire for prestige, or at least for self-worth, is universal in every society and contributes to mental health. However, the Chinese place a unique value on it and on the means of attaining it. Then the worth of an individual is regarded not in its own right but as a function of its relation to the greater collective to which one belongs. The Chinese refer to two concepts of "face," as follows.

Mien-tzu is the reputation achieved by getting on in life through worldly success and ostentation. This prestige is accumulated by means of personal effort or clever maneuvering. This kind of recognition ego is always dependent on one's external environment (a collectivist orientation). The other kind is the *lien*—that is, the group's respect for a person with a good moral reputation: the person who fulfills his or her obligations regardless of the hardships involved, who under all circumstances acts like a decent human being. It is both a social sanction for enforcing moral standards and an internalized sanction. The standards are, of course, Confucian.

When the Chinese interpretation of face is compared with that of the Westerners, like Goffman's, for example, we see that the Chinese view is more internalized and stable. Goffman (1955, p. 213) defined the term *face* as "the positive social value a person effectively claims for himself by the line others assume he has taken during a particular contact. Face is an image of self delineated in terms of approved social attributes." This concept, being situationally specific, is therefore subjected to change from situation to situation and is dependent on how well one plays the game.

If, however, an individual's face is defined by the collective of a stable society with a hierarchical order which follows a culture that has been passed on from thousands of years ago, this kind of identity is more permanent. Its influence is therefore more profound. Hsieh et al. (1969) argued that

> The individual (Chinese) in this culture tends to view his life as being relatively fixed. Luck, chance, and fate are taken for granted in life, which is considered to be full of ambiguity, complexity, and unpredictability. Life situations may be viewed as being largely determined by circumstances outside one's control (p. 122).

The Chinese Defense and Its Resolution

As a culture constrains the perceptual, explanatory, and behavioral options that individuals have at their disposal for understanding and responding to illness (Angel and Thoits, 1987), the Chinese have their own way of defining illness and seeking help. Any hint to clients that they are responsible for their own problems threatens their ability to preserve "face," and they are therefore put on the defensive. The locus of control is seen to be external to themselves, and so they tend to blame fate and misfortune. Or they may ascribe the problem to breaking the Confucian ethic.

The concept of *yuan* may serve as a buffer against any uneasiness. This concept has to do with a presumed natural affinity (destiny) for attainments in interpersonal relationships and achievements in the life of an individual. Interpersonal conflicts and under achievements are attributed to lack of "yuan." There is little the person can do about it. "Yuan," therefore, protects the "face" and the self from being scrutinized.

What happens when problems are too obvious to be defined and judged as inappropriate according to Chinese culture? Somatization is a help here. That is, the Chinese tend to believe that psychological discomfort originates in the soma. Cheung, Lee, and Chan (1983) found that given the five common physical or mental health problems faced by students—weakness and fatigue, tension and anxiety, difficulty in sleeping, "hollow-emptiness," and headache—most Chinese students initially attempt a variety of self-help measures. If the problems persist or become serious, the students first consult a medical doctor for help.

In the latter case, the students turn more to their own primary social network, namely, friends and family, in order to protect their "face" against outsiders. In accordance with Chinese folklore, family secrets should not be exposed to outsiders. When clients finally approach a mental health professional, their problems have often deteriorated massively. As Lin and Lin (1978) have observed, Chinese culture has a moral reference, whereas Americans tend to exalt the individual.

Implications for the Helping Professions

Mental health professionals in their attempt to provide services to their Chinese clients often find themselves in a maze that they must work through together to find their way out. Since counseling is designed to help clients choose a better way of life for themselves, counselors should facilitate their clients' self-understanding.

Self-actualization and self-assertiveness may provide the breakthrough for dealing with such clients. However, these terms may be too novel for the Chinese clients to comprehend. To these clients, self-actualization may mean being self-centered, and self-assertiveness may appear too dangerous for socially anxious people. Chinese clients may be too moralistic to talk frankly with even their closest friends about their real needs and frustrations.

This does not mean that genuine psychological contact cannot be established. Rather, it depends on the client's level of trust in the counselor. These are "two in one" questions that clients have to answer for themselves. Is it good to expose one's inner self to the outside world? Can the client turn his or her self to a particular counselor? Probing one's psyche directly right at the start may be too ambitious; trust has to be established first.

When the Chinese have to resolve adjustment problems, some of them turn to folk psychiatric care in the form of shamanism, divination, fortune-telling, and physiognomy, as well as traditional herbal medicine. Even though some of the more modern Chinese may doubt the validity of these practices, they often try them out in the hope of getting some inspiration as to possible solutions. Tseng (1978) has analyzed the respective functions of such practices, summed up as follows:

> Shamanism is based upon the belief that a devil or a spirit is the interfering power, and clients are taught how to cope with such *supernatural* power through exorcism or counter-magic. Divination is still based on the assumption that such supernatural power exists, and the client is supposed to learn how to live compatibly

with nature, which is ruled by this supernatural power. Fortune-telling interprets an underlying principle of *nature* that presumably rules human beings. Thus, a client is instructed how to adjust to *his nature* by following the principles of nature in order to set a matter in the right direction. Physiognomy takes the view that a *person* is predisposed to problems, and a client is taught how to *make good use of himself*. Traditional Chinese medicine tends to interpret *disharmony of internal forces or humors* and the *intrusion of external* (natural) agents as the causes of emotional disturbance, and the aim of treatment is to *regain a balanced condition* through recuperation and the supplementation and regulation of internal forces (p. 322).

Although these folk practices may not have direct effects on a particular case, when used constructively, they inspire clients to be in touch with their nature and have a clearer view of the cause of their problems. Since ideas such as "return to one's nature" and "regain a balanced condition" are advocated by these aspects of Chinese culture, they can be mediated to carry the functional equivalence of self-actualization and the holistic approach. In fact, as Chiu (1991) notes, the Daoist way to mental health is the psychological equivalence of humanistic psychology and more.

An individual's mental health status in the Daoist sense is the result of the interaction of individual characteristics with the environment. Illness is said to occur when a person becomes blind to his or her nature and reality (Chiu, 1991). Both individual needs and assertiveness have to be considered in light of the "collective" for integration and harmony. The point is not to fight nor adopt the culture blindly, but to transcend their constraints and use them to live one's life.

REFERENCES

Abel, T. M., and Hsu, F. L. K. (1949). Some aspects of personality of Chinese as revealed by the Rorschach Test. Rorschach Research Exchange and *Journal of Projective Techniques*, 13, 285–301, p. 300.

Angel, R., and Thoits, P. (1987). The impact of culture on the cognitive structure of illness. *Culture, Medicine and Psychiatry*, 11, 465–494.

Cheng, C. K. (1946). Characteristic traits of the Chinese people. *Social Forces*, 25, 146–155.

Cheung, F. M., Lee, S. Y., and Chan, Y. Y. (1983). Variations in problem conceptualizations and intended solutions among Hong Kong students. *Culture, Medicine and Psychiatry*, 7, 263–278.

The Chinese Culture Connection. (1987). Chinese values and the search for culture—free dimensions of culture. *Journal of Cross-Cultural Psychology*, 18 (2), 143–164.

Chiu, H. (1990). Theoretical and methodological issues in studying mental health amongst Chinese people. Eighth APECA Biennial Conference-Workshop paper.

Chiu, H. (1991). Mental health: a Daoist way. Conference paper, First Annual Conference on the Promotion of Mental Health. University of Keele and Mid Staffordshire Health Authority, September 1991.

Eisenberg, L. (1981). The social context of health: effects of time, place and person. In Stuart H. Fine, Robert Krell, and Tsung-yi Lin (eds.), *Today's Priorities in Mental Health: Children and Families—Needs, Rights, and Action*. London: D. Reidel Publishing Co.

Goffman, E. (1955). On face-work: an analysis of ritual elements in social interaction. *Psychiatry*, 18, 213–231.

Hofstede, G. (1980). *Culture's Consequences: International Differences in Work-related Value*. London and Beverly Hills, Calif.: Sage Publications.

Hofstede, G. (1983). Dimensions of national cultures in fifty countries and three regions. In J. B. Deregowski, S. Dziurawiec, and R. C. Annis (eds.), *Explications in Cross-cultural Psychology*, pp. 335–355. Lisse, Netherlands: Swets and Zeitlinger.

Hsieh, T. T., Shybut, J., Lotsof, E. J. (1969). Internal versus external control and ethnic group membership: a cross-cultural comparison. *Journal of Consulting and Clinical Psychology*, 33 (1), 122–124.

Hui, C. H., and Villareal, M. J. (1989). Individualism—collectivism and psychological needs: their relationships in two cultures. *Journal of Cross-Cultural Psychology*, 20 (3), 17–23.

Kahn, H. (1979). *World Economic Development: 1979 and Beyond.* London: Croom Helm.

Lin, T., and Lin, M. (1978). Service-delivery issues in Asian North American communities. *American Journal of Psychiatry*, 135, 344–453.

Tseng, W. S. (1978). Traditional and modern psychiatric care in Taiwan. In A. Kleinman (ed.), *Culture and Healing in Asian Countries: Anthropological, Psychiatric and Public Health.* New York: Cambridge University Press.

Wing, R. L. (1986). *The Tao of Power.* Wellingborough, Northamptonshire: Aquarian Press.

5. Counseling in Japan

MIKA SAITO

On March 8, 1988, the long-overdue accreditation of counselors in Japan finally went into effect, but ironically counselors can now be accredited not as counselors but as clinical psychologists. In order to understand this apparent anomaly, we must examine the status and history of counseling in Japan and how it is confused with clinical psychology.

Today, everyone in Japan has heard the word "counseling," a word that has been imported into the Japanese language. In cities commercial boards often feature marital, hair, cosmetic, and many other kinds of counseling. The word "counseling" is not used in its original meaning, however. Counselors do not know the meanings of counseling; they are only the shop assistants. In general, most people have a vague idea of counseling as some form of consultation and advice given to people in trouble. Only the few know that counseling is a way for people to consult other, knowledgeable people with regard to their psychological and mental problems.

Japan's rapid economic development in the postwar years has brought with it an increase in socio-psychological problems, such as school truancy, anorexia, bulimia, and other stress-related problems. The importance of mental health (literally in Japanese, "health of the heart") has been clearly identified. For example, Zen and Yoga, two popular forms of meditation, are taught at cultural centers, and the relaxing music that produces brain α-wave is very popular. Newspapers and other publications often carry articles about counseling. The need for and interest in counseling are widely recognized.

But what is counseling? What is its purpose and what kind of person is a subject for counseling? What exactly does a counselor do? Few people can give clear answers to any of these kinds of questions. Given the fact that its meaning is not clear even among professionals, it is not surprising that, in Japan, counseling has been slow to receive public recognition and acceptance as an independent profession. To gain a real understanding of this confusion, we must go back to the comparatively short history of counseling in Japan.

The features of counseling in Japan may be summarized as follows. Generally, the needs of counseling are increasing step by step. But in many counseling settings, such as in counseling centers, hospitals, and schools, the power of counseling is neither widespread nor accepted. The situation has not changed much in the past twenty years. Moreover, ordinary people as well as professional counselors think that counseling is the equivalent of clinical psychology. Developmental and preventive approaches are less popular than correctional and therapeutic approaches. A counselor is a clinical psychologist. The Japanese character has an influence on these situations. Ego structure in Japan is different from that of the United States and the rest of the Western world, where counseling was born. Japanese people are not self-insistent and seldom talk about what they think and feel in front of other people. Such an attitude is considered a virtue in Japan.

THE HISTORY OF COUNSELING

Counseling was a concomitant of the American occupation after World War II and began when the U.S. government sent an American educational delegation to Japan to spread the "new democratic education." In 1949 the Japanese Ministry of Education published "The Counsel for Students of Junior and Senior High School," with the course of study.

In 1951 the Advisory Committee (Chair, E. G. Williamson) of the American Council of Education sent a team of counseling experts, under the leadership of Dr. W. P. Lloyd. Their role was to lead three-month study groups on student personnel services for leaders in the field of education at the three top national universities—Tokyo, Kyoto, and Kyushu. Earlier, of course, Japan had no counselors or counseling psychologists, although there were psychiatrists and experimental psychologists, as well as some clinical psychologists. Developmental counseling at child clinics in Japan started in 1910. Also available were some kinds of counseling and psychotherapy such as Morita therapy, Naikan therapy, and Zen which were known as original Japanese counseling. Counseling was recognized as a kind of counsel or educational advice or clinical treatment for children.

In 1953 the first counseling rooms were established at Tokyo University, and in 1955 the Japanese Association of Student Counseling (formerly the Japan Student Counseling Association) was organized. In 1956 the association invited E. G. Williamson, who was followed by D. Super and C. Rogers in 1961. Later H. Borow, C. E. Thoresen, N. Kagan, A. E. Ivey, H. Pepinsky, A. Ellis, and L. Brammer were invited to its annual conference. In 1964 mental health centers were established at national universities where student counseling was included, under the leadership of the Ministry of Education, and in 1967 the Japanese Association of Counseling Science was established. This period was termed the "legend of non-directive counseling." Dr. Carl Rogers wrote *Counseling and Psychotherapy* in 1942. He called his new counseling approach "non-directive counseling" but later changed to "client-centered counseling." In the 1960s Japanese counselors believed that "nondirective counseling" was effective for all clients. When counselors only repeated the words clients said or nodded to them (people misunderstood this method as "nondirective counseling"), clients were apparently understood. So "non-directive counseling" was fashionable then. This method dominated psychotherapy in hospitals. These professionals attended study groups, and thus counseling in Japan developed in a clinical rather than in vocational or educational setting as was the case in the United States and other Western countries. Since this period, counseling services have developed in various settings in Japan, including public and private schools, universities, and industries. Now over 70 percent of all colleges and universities (from a total number of 894 national public and private universities) provide counseling services.

Counselors are educated at private training schools or training seminars in universities. A few universities offer counseling courses within an academic setting, but no overall standard and accrediting licenses existed until quite recently. In 1964 some of Japan's forty-seven prefectures organized courses in counseling or training for counselors. Tokyo prefecture, for example, organized training courses for school counselors; today two thousand senior school teachers working in Tokyo have completed this training.

During the early period, some clinical psychologists and doctors went abroad to study counseling, and they contributed to the development of counseling. Consequently, clinical psychologists in Japan were frequently seen as psychotherapists. Thus, it is not surprising that counseling in Japan, which in the West is frequently identified with psychotherapy, is identified with clinical psychology in Japan. Since the counselors were accredited in Japan, it was the clinical psychologists who were accredited.

CLINICAL PSYCHOLOGY AND COUNSELING PSYCHOLOGY IN JAPAN

The words "counseling psychology" have not been known even to professional people in Japan. Students often ask for an explanation of differences between clinical and counseling psychology. They wonder why two research institutes exist, even though they are treated as the same project. Few psychologists can answer this question correctly. Most students believe that clinical psychology is more academic than counseling psychology. The reasons why counseling psychology has not developed in Japan are as follows.

First, the therapeutic point of view can be more helpful than the developmental perspective. Japanese want to see visible effects. Second, the Japanese have been unfamiliar with preventive ways of thinking; only after something happens are countermeasures considered. Third, the Japanese lack philosophy. Counseling psychology is based on the philosophy of self-growth or self-realization, but the Japanese, favoring the technical methods, have not gotten used to it. Fourth, Japan has never had any vocational education. During childhood, boys and girls study with great diligence. Both the students and their parents are interested solely in school records, and in order to get into better schools more than 80 percent of them go to private schools. Not surprisingly, they never think of their vocation and what they will do until they are seniors in the university or have graduated from high schools. The educational system does not adapt to vocational ways of thinking.

Finally, because the educational system, the schools, and teachers are very conservative, the philosophy of counseling cannot be easily disseminated. The teacher in charge has incredibly strong influence. If the student in a particular teacher's class is sent for counseling, the teacher feels that he or she has not done enough for the student and so blames himself or herself for the situation.

THE ACADEMIC SETTING AND THE JOB

Since counseling began in 1951, many associations in related fields have been formed. For example, the Japanese Association of Counseling Science, with some 1,500 members, was formed in 1967; the Japanese Association of Student Counseling, with some 200 members, in 1964; and the Association of Japanese Clinical Psychology, with about 3,500 members, also in 1964. Although the same people often belong to these different organizations, they function independently. Their members come from many different walks of life, some are university professors, some from junior colleges or from different levels of school education, and others from clinics and hospitals, detention centers, and other social welfare agencies. Many, especially those with counseling or clinical psychology, are forced to work part-time as counselors. Although their main role might be as professors, teachers, or administrators, they are either expected to give their extra time in the counseling office of the institution or they do part-time counseling in their spare time at different institutions elsewhere.

Contrary to counseling psychology, clinical psychology has a little longer history in the academic setting. Some courses in clinical psychology have been instituted in universities, but only a few universities have doctoral courses.

Japan presently has only one graduate school that offers a degree program in counseling. It began in 1988, offering a master's degree in counseling through evening courses. There is no doctoral program. Thus, apart from the few who have done graduate studies abroad, those who are doing the counseling and those who are making the decisions with regard to accreditation have not gone through a formal university program in counseling. They have developed their own approach through reading, study groups, and personal experience.

ACCREDITATION

Because of this poor understanding and the low status of counseling in Japan, different associations have been considering accreditation for a relatively long time as a necessary protective measure for the profession. Three years after the first clinical psychologist was accredited in the United States in 1951, the Japanese government issued a document urging the development of counseling programs in education, but it was never put into practice. In 1969 the Japanese Clinical Association (now known as the Association of Japanese Clinical Psychology) was the moving force in setting up a committee to implement a system of accreditation. However, the violent eruptions on university campuses in Japan, as in other parts of the world, together with the general public's suspicion of psychology, particularly in the area of mental health, caused this process to drag on for almost twenty years. Eventually, a committee, which represented eleven different associations, came up with a system that was acceptable to all. Among the candidates for accreditation as clinical psychologists were not only counselors but also psychiatrists. The fact that both psychiatrists and counselors were accredited under the name of clinical psychologist gives some idea of the state of counseling in Japan today.

One of the major limitations of this accreditation system is that, unlike those existing for doctors and lawyers, it is not a national one. Even in such a kindred area as social welfare, a national system was established in 1990. In 1991 the accreditation was authorized by the Ministry of Education, but again it is not a national license. Discussion of accreditation was settled between the Ministry of Health and Welfare and the Ministry of Education. Moreover, because of the difficulty in defining that which relates to "health of the heart" in contrast to "health of the body," a national system is not likely in the near future. At present, those who have completed graduate studies in psychology or related fields and have had at least one to six years of clinical experience (the length of time depending on the nature of the degree itself and the area of concentration), those who apply can receive accreditation. However, they also have to present some evidence of supervision and ongoing education, by attendance at conventions, workshops, and the like.

Accreditation received is not permanent. One must apply every five years and present some evidence of having attended institutes, study groups, and so on. Herein lies the great weakness of the whole system: No objective criterion exists to judge the qualification of the person is applying for either accreditation or for re-accreditation. Bluntly put, accreditation is based not on any objective criterion, but on the ability to produce proofs of various kinds and ability to pay the rather high fee of 85,000 yen ($530). Thus far, within less than two years, some three thousand applicants have been accredited as clinical psychologists. However, the Japanese Counseling Association and other associations have their own accreditation system, although there are few applicants.

The new accreditation system has created more communication between the many interrelated associations and has helped set a basis for the ethical behavior of counselors. No longer can it be said that anyone can become a counselor. At the same time the possibility of fraudulent counselors has been lessened. Above all, a step has been taken toward formally recognizing the professionalism of counseling.

CONCLUSION

The Japanese have a great deal of difficulty in expressing their thinking and feelings to each other. In the Japanese culture, people who can guess the feelings of others without others actually divulging these feelings are highly respected. Counseling theory was born in the West and was based on the Western ego-structure. In counseling, the Japanese must develop their self-disclosure, but they find it very difficult to open their minds to others. Therefore, it is very difficult to perform counseling for the Japanese. Consequently, a way of counseling that is appropriate to Japan's culture must be found.

Implementing counseling in Japan presents many problems. First, there is an urgent need to establish counseling programs in graduate schools, with facilities and staff capable of educating and training counselors, who can obtain an M.A. or even Ph.D. in counseling. Second, it is necessary that at a national level a system be found that will objectively judge and guarantee the status and social security of those in the counseling profession. Finally, the third problem might be considered as the "software" for the "hardware" proposed in the first two problems. Ways and means must be studied and found as to what is appropriate in Japanese culture.

Today counselors in the West are interested in the Eastern cultures and in their ways of counseling such as in Yoga and Zen. Since the world community has developed and improved its communication, it is time to develop better communication with the other nations of the world.

REFERENCES

Association of Japanese Clinical Psychology. (1988). *The Manual for the Candidate of Clinical Psychologist*. Tokyo: Seishinshobo.

Hidano, S. (1989). Present society and counseling. *Japanese Journal of Counseling Science*, 22, 1–2.

Japanese Association of Student Counseling. (1988). Counselors certificate. *Newsletter*, 25.

Kawai, H. (1988). On the establishment of the Japanese Association of Clinical Psychology. *Association of Japanese Clinical Psychology Newsletter*, 10.

Murase, T. (1990). For the next ten years. *Journal of Japanese Clinical Psychology*, 9, 2.

Nakamura, H. (1988). The past, present and the future about Japanese Counseling Science. *Japanese Journal of Counseling Science*, 21, 1.

Okubo, Y. (1990a). In future of clinical psychologists. *Bulletin of Japan Society of Certified Clinical Psychologist*, 1, 1.

Okubo, Y. (1990b). *Human Mind*. Vol. 33. Japan: Hyoronsha.

Uchiyama, K. (1984). *Counseling*. Nihon Bunkakagakusya.

6. The Developmental Counseling Movement in Korea

HYUNG DEUK LEE
KI MOON SEOL

Professional counseling in Korea during the 1960s leaned heavily on medical therapeutic models (Bradley, 1978), an influence that is still very much in evidence today. According to these models, the counselor is supposed to focus on "illness" and seek to cure it in the context of an intimate doctor-patient paradigm. Counselors perceive themselves as professionals who work in an office setting and treat people who come to them with problems. In this way, counselors put themselves in a passive role and become entirely reactive rather than proactive.

By limiting their role to individual-direct-remedial services, counselors are unable to offer significant help for the mainstream of people in their community who see themselves as relatively normal. By isolating themselves from other community members, counselors who follow the therapeutic models have been losing the community's trust and have alienated themselves from the rest of the community.

Recognizing this tendency, in the late 1960s leaders of the field began to explore the role of counseling in the future and to develop new operational models for counseling professionals. Through study and revision by many groups, the developmental modes of intervention eventually emerged as an alternative to traditional medical models of counseling (Lee, 1982a). In accord with this shift, the American Personnel and Guidance Association changed its name to the American Association for Counseling and Development in 1983 (Herr, 1985).

During the 1970s developmental counseling gained prominence in the professional field, becoming a multimodal form of intervention under which the diversity of developmentally oriented models and approaches can be subsumed. Among these approaches are the student development model (T.H.E. Project, 1975), the outreach counseling model (Drum and Figler, 1976), the community psychology model (Goodyear, 1976), the community counseling model (Lewis and Lewis, 1977), the change-agent model (Paris, 1979), the ecosystem model (Task Force on Epidemiology, Campus Ecology, and the Program Evaluation, 1973). Instead of dealing with problems after they emerge, developmental counseling is devoted to the positive growth of all members in the community. Rather than confine themselves to their office and waiting, developmental counselors move out of it and become an active part of the overall community process.

The role of the developmental counselor, therefore, is to initiate, facilitate, and encourage action that will unite the community in its attempt to accomplish human developmental goals. In order to do so, developmental counselors seek to develop and implement a series of action programs for shaping forces within the community and helping community members to develop the knowledge and skills needed for personal growth, while assisting the community as a whole to become an environment that will enhance and stimulate individual development. In this way, counselors can effectively demonstrate the necessity and importance of their help to a large number of people in their community and correct the negative image associated with the remedial role they presently occupy.

Before discussing the developmental counseling movement in Korea, we will outline the brief history of counseling and examine the activities of developmental counseling in Korea. In addition, we will cover the issue of training developmental counselors.

BACKGROUND

Careful examination of the past illuminates the present and suggests the pattern of the future. The history of counseling in Korea reflects continuous change and progressive development, just as is true of other countries, especially the United States, the home of counseling. Generally, Korea's counseling history is divided into three stages: the introduction and confusion stage; the exploration stage; and the striving for professional establishment stage. However, one more stage, the introduction of developmental counseling stage, should also be included in the history.

Introduction and Confusion Stage

This stage covers the years 1945 to the mid-1950s. Korea was liberated from Japanese rule in 1945. American educational ideas, especially John Dewey's child-centered education and pragmatism in particular, were introduced to Korea, influencing the initiation of the so-called new education movement. Thus, the modern education movement in Korea is said to have begun in 1945. As mentioned above, the year 1945 marked Korea's liberation from thirty-six years of Japanese imperialistic rule.

The new education movement was to actualize the newly liberated nation's ideals based on the national spirit and democracy. Since then, Korea has adopted Hong-Ik In-Kan, Maximum Service to Humanity or Benefiting All Mankind, as the ultimate goal of its modern education. Curiously, Korea's counseling history is related to its education history, on the one hand, and to the Korean War on the other.

Unfortunately, Korea had been under Japanese control since 1905 and was liberated only in 1945 when World War II ended. However, Korea was divided into two parts, South and North, at the 38th parallel. Thus, the Korean War began as a military struggle fought between South Korea (the Republic of Korea) and North Korea (the Democratic People's Republic of Korea) on the Korean peninsula from June 1950 to July 1953. The conflict swiftly developed into a limited international war involving the United States and nineteen other nations. Those nations participated in the war as members of the United Nations. The United Nations supported the reconstruction of postwar Korea in various fields. Needless to say, counseling as well as education was among the fields supported. Specifically, a specialized U.N. agency, the Unesco-UNKRA Educational Planning Mission to Korea, led by Dr. Vester M. Mulholland, gave advice in terms of curriculum development. The guidance aspect of counseling was introduced into Korea at this time (1953).

This stage is characterized by emphasis on child welfare, humanism, and the emotional, social adjustment, and development of adolescents. Psychological testing was introduced for the first time, and intelligence testing in particular was used in counseling activities during this period, when the Korean Psychological Association was founded (1946). In fact, however, the counselor's identity was not yet established, so counselors were experiencing role confusion and were not aware of precisely what to do. Thus, the emergence of psychological testing was good news to counselors in that it created much work for them. It also had some ill effects because it led counselors to exaggerate its effect. Furthermore, it encouraged counselors to confuse psychological testing with guidance or counseling.

In 1957 the systematic counseling movement began, when the Board of Education of the city of Seoul started to train secondary school teachers as part-time counselors. By December 1961 some 170 counselors had been trained in this way. In addition, from September 1958 to July 1959 other teachers were trained in counseling by the Ministry of Education and the Central Education Institute. Even though many counselors were trained for the first time at this stage, the training itself presented some problems because counseling theory rather than practices was stressed and only foreign counseling theory, especially American theory, was introduced but without competent professional trainers. The major theory introduced at this time was Rogers' nondirective counseling theory which greatly influenced the counseling movement of Korea.

Exploration Stage

The counseling field emphasized the exploration of counseling and guidance concepts during the stage that spanned the late 1950s to late 1960s. College professors and some school counselors were concerned that counseling theory had been introduced and applied without any verification and critiques, and that they had to resort chiefly to the emotional aspect of counseling. As a result, they began to explore counseling concepts and strove to establish counseling activities. Thus, the Student Guidance Center was founded in 1962 at Seoul National University, Korea's premier university. It was followed by the establishment of other centers at other major universities throughout the country. This activity served as the momentum for the establishment of professional counseling. The textbook entitled *Principles and Practices of Guidance* by Lee and Chung (1962) and other books published during this stage systematically introduced guidance activities.

At this time, counseling classes were opened for the first time at such universities as Seoul National University and Ewha Woman's University. In addition, counseling majors at the graduate level were also opened at the same universities after a decade. The Korean Counselors Association (KCA), which consisted of junior and high school counselors, was founded in 1963. In the following year school counselors were licensed and the Ethics Committee for Psychological Testing was established, which developed counseling in earnest.

Striving for Professional Establishment Stage

This stage spanned the early 1970s to early 1980s. The counseling field aimed at professionalism starting in the 1970s, and in order to fulfill this purpose, various workshops and seminars were held throughout the country. Views of psychoanalytic, behavioral, and humanistic counseling were introduced, and the possibility of psychotherapy focusing on Zen and sensitivity training was examined.

As mentioned earlier, counseling psychology has been taught in Korea at the undergraduate level since the 1960s. However, graduate students were not able to participate in the counseling class of Ewha Woman's University until 1972. After three years, in 1975, Seoul National University offered counseling at the graduate level. The Division of Clinical Psychology (DCP) was established in the Korean Psychological Association in 1972, and the Division of Counseling Psychology and Psychotherapy (DCPP) was separated from the DCP in 1987. A credentialing program for professionals was initiated in 1973 when six members of the DCP were accredited as professional counselors. The DCPP issued the first annual *Korean Journal of Counseling and Psychotherapy* in 1989.

Most colleges and universities throughout the country managed to set up the Student Guidance Centers by the early 1970s, which enabled them to provide relatively systematic counseling services to college students. In addition, they formed the Korean College Counselors Association (KCCA) as a professional organization in 1976. The KCCA committed itself to the establishment of professional counseling through workshops, seminars, and training, introducing various counseling theories and both individual and group counseling programs. The number of professionals majoring in counseling and guidance began to increase, and the KCA held annual conventions with more than a thousand participants. The *Journal of College Counseling* has been published annually since 1990. All of these activities contributed to the professional growth of counselors in Korea.

Other incidents that led to professionalism were the legislation of the Chief School Counselor System in 1972, the adoption of ethics for counselors at the fifteenth national convention of the KCA in 1979, and the publication of various counseling books. Of special note is the introduction of group counseling during this stage. Group counseling in Korea was initiated by two different approaches in two different areas in 1971. One approach was the small-group experience based on T-group principles led by Japanese professionals of the Japanese Counselors Association. They were invited to introduce and lead the T-group for Korean counselors at Kwang Ju city, a major city in the southwestern area of Korea. This action influenced the group counseling movement, especially in Cholla province and Seoul.

The second approach was initiated by Professor Hyung Deuk Lee, who provided students of colleges and graduate schools, housewives, and Christian ministers with diverse T-group experiences. He actively introduced group counseling in terms of both theory and practice. Lee together with Professor Chang Jin Byun at the Kyungpook National University had led group counseling for four years by 1977. This activity contributed to the development of the group counseling movement in this area and throughout the country. Other events also provided important momentum for proliferating professional group counseling activities at colleges. Those were a series of KCCA's annual conventions, in 1979 and 1983, whose main topic was group counseling on college campuses.

Throughout the 1960s and 1970s Rogers' nondirective approach was the dominant influence in Korea. The secondary school counselors tended to adopt nondirective counseling and to use it in their schools.

Introduction of Developmental Counseling Stage

This stage began in 1978 when two professors initiated an informal seminar on developmental counseling. Counseling services in Korea have been offered mainly within the secondary and higher educational settings based largely on individual-direct-remedial models up until now. Generally, counselors confined themselves to listening to clients and did not engage in any other counseling activities and programs. Although all of Korea's colleges and universities had counseling centers by the early 1970s, these centers also happened to be therapy-oriented and provided individual counseling as their major function until quite recently. As a result, counseling services in Korea's schools and universities exerted little impact on the majority of the student population, and the educators, administrators, and parents tended to view counseling as unimportant.

In this situation, developmental counseling was introduced into Korea in 1978 when two university professors, Drs. Hyung Deuk Lee and Chang Jin Byun, who had just returned from the United States with degrees in counseling, initiated an informal seminar on developmental counseling with several graduate students from both Kyungpook National University and Keimyung University in Taegu, Korea. The meetings were held every Friday evening, so that the meetings themselves were called Friday Meetings, and lasted for about four years. At first, the meetings started with small-group experiences that focused on the personal growth of participants in order to develop human resources for the new counseling movement. In addition, study sessions on such topics as recent trends in guidance and counseling, outreach in counseling, organizational change, and community development were included to equip the movement with sufficient theoretical background.

On the other hand, some developmental classes were opened for the first time at the college level, especially at Keimyung University, actively influenced by Dr. Hyung Deuk Lee. For example, the subject of human relations was opened as a general education subject for freshmen, and specially trained faculty members held a special class named the Open Seminar for all freshmen every week. This seminar provided growth experiences. In addition, the subject of human relations was also opened at the graduate level.

In 1982 a society for the study of developmental counseling was organized as the predecessor of a formal association. At the same time, Personal Growth Programs which provided growth-group experience and leader training were opened to the public. The

Korean Association of Developmental Counseling (KADC) was eventually founded in 1986. In 1988 the association opened an attached counseling center. It was named the Developmental Counseling Center (DCC) to signify a basic change in direction and philosophy; developmental and preventative counseling interventions were now emphasized.

The DCC was approved as a corporation in 1990. Developmental counseling activities provided by the KADC and DCC are described in the next section.

DEVELOPMENTAL COUNSELING ACTIVITIES

To help change the image of the traditional counseling services and to reflect a new philosophy and direction in the counseling field, KADC has been emphasizing the design and implementation of new programs and services during the past decade. Consequently, several new programs were developed and implemented in various settings such as secondary schools, colleges and universities, business organizations, and the overall community. Examples of these programs are the personal growth group (Yoon and Lee, 1980), human relations training (Lee, 1982b), assertiveness training (Byun and Kim, 1980), study-skill training (Kim, 1987), values clarification training (Lee, 1984), shyness overcoming programs (Seol, 1989), happiness programs (Seol, 1990), and family counseling programs (Kim, 1990).

Koreans experienced drastic social, political, and economic changes after the 1980s. In terms of economy, gross national product has increased, so that Korea's overall economic conditions improved greatly. Thus, past authoritarianism has been rejected in the various fields of society, and democratic ways have been pursued.

As the Bible says, "man does not live by bread alone." Today many Koreans, including workers, are adding, "Nor does he work for bread alone, at least not anymore." Thus, there is a growing realization that the employees of today are indeed a new breed.

They appear to have different values, different needs, and different motivations than their predecessors. They are better educated, a product of the knowledge explosion, more aware politically, socially, and economically, more demanding, less easily managed by traditional controls, and generally more sophisticated. The KADC, realizing the necessity of focusing on this new breed, has endeavored to develop human resources programs in the industrial setting. Examples of those programs designed and implemented for business organizations are human relations training, personal growth group programs, T-group experience, and leader effectiveness training. Since the overall response to these programs is very positive, they are increasingly applied to a wider population in the business organizations.

Korean education has experienced a lot of difficulties as a necessary consequence of its stress on intellectual development for college entrance at the cost of education of the whole person. Thus, students have been forced to stay at school all day long and as such are given few opportunities for affective and human experiences and for development as psychologically mature persons. Thus, they have a difficult time forming identities, establishing self-concepts, and actualizing themselves. As a result, many social problems, including juvenile delinquency, for example, have surfaced. The government and community institutions have made a concerted effort both to prevent and to correct these problems. Since it is believed that all parents, teachers, and community members should be aware of the seriousness of the problem in order to cope with juvenile delinquency, the KADC developed programs for parents, teachers, and community members concerned as well as for students.

In addition, the KADC served academic community members and laypersons in terms of seminars, special lectures, and group counseling sessions in the developmental counseling field. For example, the KADC twice held a national series of special lecture meetings. First, in 1988 a national meeting was held in commemoration of opening the DCC, and the following topics were presented: counseling and social services, mentally healthful thinking, and the nature of developmental counseling. Another national meeting, whose main topic was the functions and roles of the Community Counseling Center, was held in 1991 in commemoration of DCC's approval as a corporation. The subtitles presented at this meeting were the counseling activities of the community counseling center, the education and training activities of the community counseling center, and the research activities of the community counseling center.

The DCC has offered public outreach, developmental counseling seminars, named the Thursday Seminar, to community members every Thursday since 1989. The first seminar, held in 1989, was devoted to human relations and it continued for two semesters. In addition, such topics as parent effectiveness training and understanding of developmental psychology have been presented. The services offered by the KADC and DCC reflect the urgent needs of the present Korean society and the counseling field. Since KADC has about thirty members and DCC has only a limited number of staff, almost all members of the KADC have been expected to serve as voluntary part-time counselors. For the members, however, the opportunities for involvement have enabled them to develop further skills, enhance their professional development, feel more competent in their services, and meet a wider range of public needs. Furthermore, the KADC could be led to implement broader outreach modes of counseling interventions so as to increase its impact of the whole community. Thus, the KADC and the DCC have been increasingly able to win public recognition from the community along with the passage of time.

In addition, Korea has several more developmentally oriented counseling organizations—for example, the Growth Counseling Center, the Psychological Counseling Center of Korea, the Human Development Institute in Seoul, the Paek-Jang-Am Temple, which provides the so-called Tong-Sa-Sup encounter group counseling in Cholla province, and the Cha-Gong Psychological Counseling Center in Pusan City. These organizations are also rendering developmental modes of counseling services to their communities through a wide variety of activities and programs, including sensitivity training, spiritual growth groups, human relations training, stress management, parent effectiveness training, marriage enrichment, and lectures on mental health. Furthermore, the Korean Ministry of Education initiated a special program, the Mother Volunteer Counselor System, in Seoul in 1985. After pilot experimentations for three years, it has been expanded throughout the major cities since 1988.

Especially noteworthy is the development of diverse telephone counseling services in the last decade. Those services are open to community members, including children, adolescents, adults, workers, women, and senior citizens, and they are provided either by telephone counseling agencies or by social welfare institutions and community centers. Either way, these services are rendered chiefly by paraprofessional volunteers.

The other developmental outreach mode of counseling services recently offered in the major cities in the psycho-education program, which is composed of sensitivity training and psychodrama. This special program is supported by the National Police Headquarters for juvenile delinquents. Even though it is very limited, it has had a positive effect. Peer counseling services offered by students at several major universities is another example of the activities of developmental counseling. Peer leaders work for hundreds of students, providing group counseling experiences and other helpful services in the peer counseling system. Thus, it can be concluded that the developmental counseling movement in Korea has been making steady progress and is extending its impact throughout the whole country.

TRAINING DEVELOPMENTAL COUNSELORS

In order to work with and provide assistance to the majority of people in their community, developmental counselors need to develop ways of multiplying their effect on people (Drum and

Figler, 1976). Many counselors are presently working at or beyond their capacity to provide services. The prospects of serving three or four times as many people would seem to be an overwhelming task. How can the counselor then assist the majority of the people? Part of the answer lies in finding additional sources of help, such as people with potential to become paraprofessionals or nonprofessionals within the community. As suggested by Brown (1974) and Tindall (1989), the emergence of nonprofessionals or paraprofessionals is the direct result of both an increasing demand for counseling services and the inability of professionally trained personnel to provide all of these services. In this sense, training in the developmental counseling field should deal with paraprofessionals as well as professionals.

The Training of Professionals

The major training courses/programs for professionals are found in colleges or universities, since higher educational institutions can offer a variety of academic resources and a traditional means of obtaining credits, degrees, and credentials (Lewis and Lewis, 1977). However, the typical program for training professionals in Korea is the graduate course. Even though there are many graduate courses in the counseling field in Korea, few schools have developmentally oriented programs. For example, Keimyung University has two kinds of developmentally oriented graduate programs: the counseling program of the graduate school leading to the Ph.D. and M.A. degrees, and that of the graduate school of education leading to the M.Ed. degree. These programs were organized and developed to train developmentally oriented professionals.

Apprenticeships in the counseling field are not as yet well developed in Korea. Generally, counseling institutions have credit-granting programs in the United States; as yet, no institution in Korea has any such program. Apprenticeships are sometimes provided by the counseling center attached to a university and the counseling agencies within the community. The Division of Coun-

seling Psychology and Psychotherapy of the Korean Psychological
Association recently established an intensive training system for
professionals. As a result, the first training program was offered
for ten days in the summer of 1991.

The Training of Paraprofessionals

When people first become aware of their problems and seek
assistance, they often tend to ask for the help of people other than
professional counselors. An individual can ease into a problem by
mentioning it to a friend before he considers taking the more
difficult step of seeing a counselor. Thus, the importance of
utilizing people other than professionals is stressed in developmental counseling (Drum and Figler, 1976).

In any community, a number of people function on an informal
basis in helping roles. Thus, one important role that the developmental counselor can perform is to identify those people who have
the ability, interest, and perhaps some experience that may qualify
them to help individuals satisfy their developmental needs. These
are people with helping potential. Another important role undertaken by the developmental counselor is to train them. These
trained people with helping potential may be called paraprofessionals or nonprofessionals. The paraprofessionals are those who
support professional counselors by taking over clerical tasks and
the lower end of the problem hierarchy (test interpretation, advis-
ing, etc.); they have been utilized for some time. Paraprofessionals
also function as counselor aides, lay helpers, and peer counselors.
They are widely utilized in such various settings as schools and
universities, community centers, religious organizations, business
organizations, and hospitals.

The DCC provides group counseling services through which
people are trained to become effective paraprofessionals. Paraprofessionals get help through three kinds of group counseling services divided into a primary level, an intermediate level, and an

advanced level for leaders. All levels are operated on the basis of personal growth principles.

There are also outreach-mode training programs for industrial personnel. The Korean industrial community has experienced severe labor-management disputes for about a decade. Thus, most companies have considered counterplans and have instituted programs for overcoming difficulties. Typical programs are counseling-type training programs for staff, managers, and workers. The contents of the programs are interview-skill training, counseling skill, human relations training, leadership training, sensitivity training, group counseling, organization development, and team-building skill training. The trained staffs have been utilized as peer counselors or group counseling leaders. As far as the DCC is concerned, it has most frequently offered training services to the Lucky-Gold Star Group, one of the typical large financial groups in Korea. Similarly, other companies have invested much money in getting help in the counseling-type training field.

CONCLUSION

The history of counseling in Korea is not long enough to have established a tradition. Nevertheless, counseling has good prospects, particularly in terms of developmental counseling. Counseling trends have shifted from the passive therapeutic approach to the active developmental approach. Hyung Deuk Lee (1982) maintained the necessity of developmental counseling in "Theoretical Background and Recent Trends of College Student Guidance," which he presented at a national academic symposium. In the same year, Chang Ho Lee (1982) also suggested the possibility of expanding the role of developmental counseling. In addition, other authors such as Park (1986), Hong (1986), and Lee (1988) introduced the need for developmental counseling and related activities in their books. The eleventh annual convention of the KCCA, held in 1988, proposed such topics as the counselor's new role in student development. The participants discussed this topic in terms of developmental counseling. As a result, many university student guidance centers offered various developmental counseling programs in addition to therapeutic individual counseling and psychological testing services. For example, they utilized peer counselors and communication training programs.

Before further progress is possible, developmental counseling in Korea must overcome several difficult obstacles. First, employment opportunities for professionals are limited. Even though counseling agencies have been increasingly established in communities in recent years, they are generally operated by part-time paraprofessional volunteers rather than professionals since economic conditions for hiring full-time professionals are not good enough. Thus, the quality of services has frequently been questionable. Although they are trained for some time before employment, more training is needed for good-quality services for clients. At any rate, professionals have a hard time finding appropriate job opportunities.

Second, many counseling agencies have been established not by professionals but by laypersons who are improperly trained or without training and educational background in the counseling field. Thus, they don't fully realize the importance of counseling services for the community. In order for counseling agencies to render good services to clients, they should be operated by professionals approved by the academic community and the authorities concerned. The government should support them in many ways, including economically and administratively.

Third, more comprehensive developmental counseling programs should be developed. Although many programs have been established and applied to various settings so far, more efforts should be devoted to developing the programs. Accordingly, need assessments of the clients should be required. It is generally recognized that the need is a gap between a current set of circumstances and some changes toward a desirable set of circumstances. Thus, the need assessment is a measuring and appraising of the gap between the current situation and the desirable set of circumstances. Proper techniques should be developed and applied for this purpose.

Fourth, the developmental aspects of counselor education and training should receive greater emphasis. Although many colleges and universities have counseling programs in their graduate schools, those programs do not reflect the needs of developmental counseling in school, society, and community. Thus, many professionals are not fully aware of the needs, theory, and practices of developmental counseling and are not successful in meeting the clients' developmental needs. Although developmental counseling in Korea has encountered some problems, it is strongly believed that these will be solved in the near future.

REFERENCES

Bradley, M. K. (1978). Counseling past and present: is there a future? *Personnel and Guidance Journal*, 57, 42–45.

Brown, W. F. (1974). Effectiveness of paraprofessionals: the evidence. *Personnel and Guidance Journal*, 53(4), 257–264.

Byun, C. J., and Choo, S. H. (1980). A communication skills training program for high school peer counselors. *Journal of Student Guidance* (Kyungpook National University), 13, 1–85 (in Korean).

Byun, C. J., and Kim, S. H. (1980). An assertiveness training program. *Journal of Student Guidance* (Kyungpook National University), 13, 51–85 (in Korean).

Drum, D. J., and Figler, H. E. (1976). *Outreach in Counseling*. Cranston, R.I.: Carroll Press.

Goodyear, R. K. (1976). Counselors as community psychologists. *Personnel and Guidance Journal*, 54, 512–516.

Herr, E. L. (1985). AACD: an association committed to unity through diversity. *Journal of Counseling and Development*, 63, 395–404.

Hong, K. J. (1986). *Guidance for Growth*. Seoul: Tam Gu Dang (in Korean).

Kim, N. O. (1987). A study skill training program I: reading skills. *Journal of Student Guidance* (Kyungpook National University), 20, 57–87 (in Korean).

Kim, S. N. (1990). "A model of family counseling by means of sequential interventions in personal, interpersonal, and family-unit levels of family system." Unpublished Ph.D. diss., Keimyung University (in Korean).

Lee, C. H. (1982). *Introduction to Counseling*. Seoul: Park Yong Sa Publishing Co. (in Korean).

Lee, H. D. (1982a). The recent trends and theoretical background in guidance and counseling. *Guidance and Counseling* (Keimyung University), 7, 1–17 (in Korean).

Lee, H. D. (1982b). *Human Relations Training*. Seoul: Joong Ang Juk Sung Chool Pan Sa (in Korean).

Lee, J. C. (1988). *Guidance*. Seoul: Moon Um Sa Publishing Co. (in Korean).

Lee, S. Y. (1984). A values clarification program. *Guidance and Counseling* (Keimyung University), 9, 49–76 (in Korean).

Lee, Y. D., and Chung, W. S. (1962). *Principles and Practices of Guidance*. Seoul: Kyo Yuk Kwa Hak Sa (in Korean).

Lewis, J. A., and Lewis, M. D. (1977). *Community Counseling: A Human Services Approach*. New York: John Wiley and Sons.

Paris, C. (1979). *The Counselor as Change Agent*. Ann Arbor, Mich.: Eric Counseling and Personnel Services Clearinghouse.

Park, S. S. (1986). *Guidance*. Seoul: Chung Min Sa Publishing Co. (in Korean).

Seol, K. M. (1982). Training for overcoming shyness. Translated from P. G. Zimbardo and S. L. Radl (1979). *The Shyness Workbook*. Seoul: Hyungsol Publishing Co. (in Korean).

Seol, K. M. (1990). A group counseling program for increasing personal happiness. *Research Review* (Dong-A University), 19, 45–65 (in Korean).

Task Force on Epidemiology, Campus Ecology, and Program Evaluation, Western Interstate Commission for Higher Education, the Ecosystem Model: Designing Campus Environments. Boulder, Colo.: Western Interstate Commission for Higher Education (1975).

T.H.E. Project. (1975). A student development model for student affairs in tomorrow's education. *Journal of College Student Personnel*, 16, 334–341.

Tindall, J. A. (1989). *Peer Counseling: An In-Depth Look at Training*

Peer Helpers, 3rd ed. Muncie, Ind.: Accelerated Development Inc.

Yoon, H. S., and Lee, H. D. (1980). A learning program for personal growth. *Guidance and Counseling* (Keimyung University), 1–46 (in Korean).

7. Counseling and Guidance in New Zealand

MARGARET E. HENSHAW

Counseling and guidance in New Zealand has had a somewhat haphazard history. Initiatives were first taken by a variety of people working in private organizations: the Young Men's Christian Association (YMCA), government departments such as education and welfare, and university departments of education and philosophy. The degree of cooperation and integration of efforts has varied, from little or none to considerable, depending on individual inclination and effort rather than on regulation and central organization. The field has experienced periods of growth and enthusiasm, such as in the 1960s and 1970s, and periods when the profession has been forced to redefine and redirect itself because of social conditions and governmental changes, as happened during the 1980s.

In New Zealand the term *counselor* is used in numerous contexts, some of which are specific and professional, and others which have no professional context. Training falls into three broad groups: those with university postgraduate training; those with well-organized integrated training, often in voluntary organizations; and those with a variety of skills, sometimes on a high level, acquired through their attendance at short courses and from their own life experiences. Historically, employment opportunities have been restricted to a few specific areas, but well-trained, skilled people are now finding employment in a much wider range of occupations.

New Zealand is going through a difficult economic time, which has created a range of social and employment problems that are being dealt with by a decreasing number of both paid and voluntary workers. Many problems and issues have resulted from economic restructuring. A major issue for both counselors and New Zealand society as a whole is how it faces up to biculturalism and the creation of a truly bicultural society.

New Zealand has two main cultures, European or Pakeha (Maori for "pale skin") and Maori, the original Polynesian settlers. The European cultural traditions have dominated most aspects of society. The future directions and prospects of counseling in New Zealand may well depend on how well individuals and society meet the challenges inherent in life in New Zealand society in the 1990s.

SOCIAL AND HISTORICAL BACKGROUND

Historically, the impetus for counseling services came from two directions: vocation and mental retardation. First, groups such as the YMCA recognized the need for young men initially, and later young women, to continue their education into secondary school. During the late 1920s the YMCA established vocational guidance centers "for the purposes of educational and vocational guidance, placement, followup, and help in planning leisure time activities" (Winterbourn, 1974). During the next twenty years, this initiative was followed by appointments of vocational guidance staff in the technical colleges, and government officially recognized vocational guidance. The social conditions of the time gave extra impetus: the economic depression meant that large numbers of people of all ages were out of work, and a few years later, during World War II, many women replaced men in the workforce. After the war, the retraining and readjustment problems were accompanied by a growing social and educational sophistication, and the beginnings of industrial developments and rural problems, which assumed major proportions in the 1950s (Winterbourn, 1974).

The second direction of development came from specific individuals within the education and philosophy departments of New Zealand universities. These people were concerned with "behavioral problems, backward children, the diagnosis of educational retardation and treatment" (Winterbourn, 1974: 6). Clinics were established in some universities where both primary and secondary school children were clinically assessed and counseled. "The great majority came for intellectual assessment and educational guidance, and a smaller but significant number came as a result of problems associated with general or specific backwardness, behavior, and delinquency" (Winterbourn, 1974: 21). From this initiative, the Psychological Service developed, and because of changing social conditions, it was pressured to remain primarily a center for remedial treatment.

School counseling began to develop through the appointment of career counselors and visiting teachers in the late 1940s. In the postwar years New Zealand saw major social changes, which resulted in the schools becoming "increasingly concerned about problems of juvenile delinquency and moral standards, truancy, and other social problems" (Winterbourn, 1974: 78). The first secondary school counselors were appointed in 1966, and their work was to include three main areas: educational guidance, vocational guidance, and personal counseling. By 1992 all secondary schools with more than four hundred pupils had a guidance counselor.

Tertiary educational institutions have slowly developed student services sections which include counseling staff. The work done in counseling centers varies, but most centers emphasize one-to-one counseling, supported by group program.

Increased unemployment and the attendant social stress of the last five years have seen an increasing demand for counseling services and a decrease in their funding. Financial assistance to voluntary organizations has been cut back. Restructuring the Labour Department has caused the redeployment of vocational counselors to other positions, and changes in staffing allowances at secondary schools have meant the loss of some counseling positions.

DEFINITIONS

In New Zealand the term *counseling* was originally used predominantly to refer to counseling and guidance in relation to those working in careers or vocational guidance areas. The New Zealand Counseling and Guidance Association was formed in 1974, and its membership was drawn primarily from those people working in secondary schools as guidance counselors and career advisers. In 1990 the Association decided on a name change to the New Zealand Association of Counselors (Te Ropu Kaiwhiriwhiri o Aotearoa). This change reflects the reduced emphasis on guidance in schools and the increase in individual counseling in both the schools and the community. The membership of the Association now includes counselors working in a wide variety of community organizations, schools, tertiary institutions, and private practice. There are no regulations governing the practice of counselors, but members of the Association do have a code of practice. However, anyone can set up practice, call himself or herself a counselor, and charge a fee.

TRAINING

Practicing counselors can take advantage of three main forms of training: in university postgraduate training, which involves either a diploma in counseling or a master of counseling degree; organized training program undertaken by volunteer workers, such as marriage guidance counseling training; and practical experience supported by a variety of short courses offered by polytechnics and community organizations.

University Training

To be accepted into a diploma or master of counseling course at a New Zealand university, students undergo a selection process. The courses last a minimum of two years and offer a mix of theoretical and practical knowledge and skills. These training programs began in 1973 in response to the expansion of the guidance roles in schools during the 1960s and early 1970s (Webster and Hermansson, 1983). They have changed and developed in relation to change in the range and diversity of the backgrounds and potential employment areas of students studying in them.

Volunteer Workers' Programs

Historically, volunteers have provided counseling in the community. The economic pressures of the last few years have produced a number of changes in the funding of voluntary organizations. Volunteers still make a significant contribution to the counseling available. Such organizations have developed their own training program specific to their particular needs. These programs are skills-based and usually involve on-the-job training, with supervision and workshop training leading to accreditation within the organization. Examples of such organizations are Marriage Guidance, Lifeline, and Rape Crisis.

Short Courses and Practical Experience

Short courses lasting from eight to thirty hours are offered by polytechnics and a variety of community-based organizations. Practicing and potential counselors use these courses to enhance already existing skills or to develop skills in new areas. Many people find themselves in positions, either paid or voluntary, that are not specifically for counseling but where the use of basic counseling skills is almost fundamental to the position.

EMPLOYMENT OPPORTUNITIES

Historically, counselors have been in paid employment in secondary schools as guidance counselors and in the Labour Department as vocational counselors. Volunteer counselors have often moved into paid positions where their counseling skills have been a valuable asset.

Since the late 1980s, New Zealand has experienced considerable economic and social restructuring, a process that has been painful and distressing for many individuals and families. Counseling services have been in even greater demand at a time when funding to voluntary groups has been ever more difficult to secure. Consequently, paid counseling positions have been established in some organizations, but now a charge has been instituted for services that, until now, have been provided by donation or free. Ironically, while paid employment has resulted for a few people, counseling has been put beyond the means of many who are most in need.

Today New Zealand also has counselors who work in private practice, and increasingly, counselors are finding employment where counseling skills are a requirement of the position, in addition to other skills such as administration and educational promotion. Counselors have been employed in areas such as alcohol and drug dependence, the AIDS Foundation, women's health, and sexual abuse and healing centers.

While counselors are happy about their paid employment and the recognition of their skills, this employment may also be a significant comment on the society New Zealand has become. A significant proportion of New Zealanders have expressed the feeling that they don't "belong" in mainstream society. Counselors have described their employment dilemma:

> The problem we face is that to a large extent our "belonging" is a function of others "not belonging." The larger this body of people is, the more likely we are to feel we have a place and to be treated likewise. The issue, though, is who governs what that place will be? It is my belief that if we ever reach the point where we feel we

totally belong, we had better take a good look at what sort of a society we have and what we are doing to sustain it (Hermansson, 1990).

CHALLENGES, PROBLEMS, AND ISSUES

The most significant challenge to counseling, as well as to many other educational and social situations in New Zealand, is how to address the issues involved in developing a truly bicultural approach to counseling. Most institutions and organizations have recognized the challenge, and some have made changes in training programs. The Marriage Guidance (Waikato) policy states: "We will provide the resources and support for Maori people to develop their own counseling center." TeKorowhai Aroha is now a fully independent counseling center for Maori people. This approach could provide part of the answer. Nevertheless, it remains imperative that Pakeha counselors use their best counseling skills to listen to what Maori people are saying and begin to move their cultural boundaries to more appropriately assist the people they work with.

The issue of culturally appropriate counseling is fundamental to all aspects of counseling: the individual counselor and his or her relationship to the client, the institution in which the counselor works, the training that is offered and that which is recognized as professional training for employment purposes, and acceptance into professional organizations that represent the counseling profession.

Counselors in New Zealand are predominantly white and middle class.

If culture is defined so as to include economic and social as well as ethnic cultures, then most of the challenges, problems, and issues facing counseling are issues of culture. The solutions will not be easy either to discover or to implement, but if members of the profession are serious about a genuine bicultural society, then counselors must take up this challenge positively as individuals, in their professional organizations, and in education and training programs.

FUTURE DIRECTIONS AND PROSPECTS

The increasing complexities and pressures of life in New Zealand suggest that counselors will play a continuing and probably increasing role. What form this role takes will depend on individuals, the training they are given, and the form of employment they are expected to fulfill.

The demand for one-to-one counseling can come into conflict with the desire of many counselors to work in a more preventive, educative way. Ideally, the two approaches should complement each other. The provision of enough counselors to meet the need for individual counseling is unlikely ever to be met by either paid or voluntary workers. Hence, counselors constantly need to review the therapeutic models that they use and to consider alternatives to lengthy, one-to-one work where possible. Above all, it is imperative that those involved in counseling consider ways that they either contribute to or challenge the society and system that creates the ever-increasing need for counseling services.

REFERENCES

Hermansson, G. (1990). It won't be long: counselling and guidance poised for the nineties. In John Small and Tony Ambrose (eds.), *Counselling and Guidance Towards the Nineties*. Palmerston North: New Zealand Counselling and Guidance Association.

Webster, A. C., and Hermansson, G. L. (1983). Guidance and counseling in New Zealand. *The Personnel and Guidance Journal*, 61 (8), 472–475.

Winterbourn, R. (1974). *Guidance Services in New Zealand Education*. Wellington: New Zealand Council for Educational Research.

8. Counseling in Australian Higher Education

MARGARET ROBERTSON

Counseling services are well established in Australia's higher education. Founded nearly forty years ago in a period of generous educational expansion, the profession initially enjoyed a vigorous period of growth, establishing a hybrid model of practice that owed much to U.S. and British influences. Financial stringencies and changing educational policies have dictated processes of contraction and consolidation over the last decade, producing tougher times for counselors. There is evidence, however, that a more mature integrated model of practice has emerged, one that is more closely attuned to Australian conditions and the goals and needs of higher education in the 1990s. Over its history the developing profession has been characterized by liveliness and debate, and there is every evidence that this tradition is continuing.

Counseling in higher education in Australia is a profession without a strong tradition of research and review. There are no current comprehensive statistics on the field. The only major review that has been undertaken is that of student services conducted by Ernest Roe and his colleagues in 1980–1981 (Roe et al., 1982). This chapter draws on their report where appropriate, and I gratefully acknowledge this source. The overall point of view expressed here is a personal one, however, based on eighteen years of involvement as a counselor in higher education.

CURRENT PROVISION OF
COUNSELING SERVICES

All universities and most colleges in Australia employ counselors, usually within a student services organization. They are predominantly qualified counseling psychologists, and their duties could broadly be described as those of providing personal, educational, and vocational counseling. However, their duties vary with the size of the institution and service in which they are employed. Counselors in smaller colleges tend to be sole practitioners, and they are frequently expected to assume responsibility for assisting with such basic student concerns as housing and financial aid, in addition to their professional counseling responsibilities. By contrast, counselors in larger colleges and universities may be employed in a department of up to eight counselors. In these situations, a comprehensive network of student services attends to basic student needs, including health services, financial aid and welfare assistance, housing services, careers and employment services, and chaplaincy. Thus, the counselors are free to specialize in psychological counseling for students and sometimes staff, and usually they also conduct educational group programs. They may provide consultation to their institutions and engage in research. In these well-staffed services, a provision of one counselor for about three thousand enrolled students is achieved. In the worst situations, it can be as high as one to ten thousand students. Individual institutions determine what proportion of their budget will be devoted to student and counseling services. Thus, great diversity exists, and generalizations can be made only with caution.

HIGHER EDUCATION IN AUSTRALIA

Higher education in Australia is noteworthy for its diversity. This results from the fact that Australia is a large country with an unevenly distributed population, and colleges and universities have been established in response to local need. The involvement of two levels of government in higher education administration has resulted in the existence of two sectors—the University and Colleges of Advanced Education (CAE) sector, administered by the Commonwealth government, and the Technical and Further Education sector (TAFE), the responsibility of the state governments.

The universities have traditionally been regarded as the elite institutions, focusing on research and scholarship and enrolling students with the highest academic talent. Some have histories dating back to the nineteenth century. By contrast, most CAEs were established during the period of great educational expansion in Australia in the 1960s and 1970s or developed out of earlier technical or teacher training institutions during that period. While most have conferred equivalent-level qualifications to those awarded by the universities, they have largely been accorded lower status. They have concentrated on offering vocationally oriented courses, often with strong industrial links.

These distinctions, never absolute, became increasingly blurred in the 1980s and have now all but disappeared in the wake of the Commonwealth government's recent radical restructuring of higher education. Amalgamations of universities and CAEs have been directed and largely achieved, resulting in the simplified National Unified System. Traditional funding differentials have been removed; research funds are no longer the preserve of universities but are available for competitive bidding from all tertiary institutions. All are expected to contribute to scholarship and to provide vocational education relevant to the needs of the Australian economy. The balance to be achieved varies only with an institution's particular profile and established areas of expertise. Facilitation of equitable access to higher education for the broad Australian community is a high priority objective for all.

TAFE colleges were originally founded as extensions of secondary education in order to provide basic vocational training for those entering trades and other areas of skilled employment. In recent years, they have diversified into a broader range of technical, scientific, and business areas and have raised the level of their courses, but their emphasis on practical skills remains. In some cases upper level TAFE courses overlap with those of the universities and CAEs, and articulation arrangements between the two sectors are receiving particular attention. This is because TAFEs frequently constitute an entry point into higher education for educationally and economically disadvantaged groups in the community.

SOCIAL AND HISTORICAL BACKGROUND OF COUNSELING SERVICES

In order to understand the current operations and objectives of the higher education counseling services, it is necessary to be aware of their history and the various influences on their development. I am indebted to the Roe report in framing this history (Roe et al., 1982).

Establishment of Counseling Services

The advent of counseling services in Australian higher education dates from the expansion of university education in the decade immediately following World War II. Prior to this time, there was apparently no perception of a need for counselors. Universities existed to provide education in a highly predictable form to a small, relatively homogeneous elite in the population. They were modeled on the British university tradition and, accordingly, the roles of teacher and student were well defined. Students relied on their teachers, tutors, and residential college chaplains and staff for assistance and guidance.

But this closed predictable system suddenly underwent rapid dislocation. The influx of returning servicemen and women seeking the new lives and educational opportunities they had been promised began to alter the university population. In addition, the apparently strong need for a better educated workforce to achieve postwar reconstruction dictated that the talented and educable members of the populace be identified and the universities expanded to accommodate them. Able students from families that hitherto had had no access to higher education appeared on campuses. They were assisted and encouraged by competitive scholarships and teaching traineeships. This new heterogeneous population with widely differing backgrounds, aptitudes, and aspirations soon revealed a need for guidance and assistance that teaching staffs could no longer accommodate. Specialist advisors, at first part-time, were appointed on campuses. The role of the university counselor was born.

The first full-time position of student counselor was established in 1953 at Melbourne University, and by 1960 seven of the nine existing universities employed counselors. The reports of government commissions established to oversee the great higher education expansion endorsed the appointment of counselors, and, as new universities and CAEs were established or upgraded over the next two decades, counselors were almost routinely appointed. When Roe and his colleagues surveyed student services in 1980–1981, they reported 100 percent coverage of personal counseling functions in universities and 97 percent in the CAEs (Roe et al., 1982).

Attention to the TAFE sector came a little later, starting in 1974. Unfortunately for TAFE, this was the decade when expansionary expenditures on higher education in Australia slowed to a halt. Government reports were no less enthusiastic in recommending counselor appointments for TAFE, but the level of funding was never made available to match the provision in the universities and CAEs. While counselors were appointed, it is predominantly in TAFE where counselors today are likely to be sole practitioners, carrying a wide range of general responsibilities in the area of student services.

Government's Rationale for Counseling Services

From the beginning, the government's rationale for supporting the establishment of counseling services focused squarely on the issue of reducing attrition rates among students. For example, in

1957 the Murray Committee expressed alarm at the failure rates among the highly selected Commonwealth Scholarship holders. Assistance with adjustment, transition, and development of academic skills was prescribed as the remedy. The Australian Vice-Chancellors Committee (AVCC) conference in 1960 recommended that the government extend counseling services. The committee described its functions at that time as

> assistance to students with problems of adaptation to university, assistance to students in developing efficient habits of study, including in some cases provision of special services such as reading improvement training, vocational guidance of students and intending students, counseling in problems of minor psychological disturbance, liaison with secondary schools, liaison with community medical and psychiatric services (AVCC, 1960, p. 52).

By 1972 the third report of the Commission on Advanced Education persuasively argued the cost/benefit role of supportive services for students, concluding: "we regard the need for supportive services as being beyond dispute if waste is to be minimized" (Commission on Advanced Education, 1972, 7.31).

Again in 1975 the sixth report of the Universities Commission contained the following endorsement:

> The Commission recognizes that personal and welfare counseling services play a valuable role in overcoming problems of student adjustment to university life and in improving academic performance. The Commission wishes to encourage universities which already provide these services to extend them, and those universities which do not have them to introduce them and make them widely available. It believes that the universities are funded at a level which will permit appropriate development of such services (Universities Commission, 1975, 11.13).

How Counseling Services Developed

When we read these early governmental reports, it is hard to imagine a professional group being given a stronger or clearer mandate for its operations than that given to higher education counseling. After reviewing its development, therefore, it is perhaps surprising to chart the directions that were taken and to uncover a continuing theme of controversy and uncertainty among the counselors about what they should actually be doing and attempting to achieve. That their most recent professional gathering was under the conference theme "Redefining Our Relevance," in Sydney in January 1991 indicates that this uncertainty persists to the present day. [1]

Many of the early counseling services closely conformed to the government's objectives. Counselors were expected to possess teaching qualifications and experience and to administer selection and aptitude tests. Classes in study skills and sometimes speed reading were conducted. Guidance tended to be rather directive, in keeping with the counselors' teaching backgrounds. A conference paper describing the work of a counseling service in a CAE at this period portrayed a counselor who believed he knew what was best for the student, "subtly and unobtrusively steering the conversation towards some positive objective" (Niemann, 1965: 5). The title of this paper, "Each to His Full Stature. The Discovery and Development of Individual Talent: The Role of the Student Counsellor," nicely illustrates the educational values of the period.

A shift in the operations of counseling services began to be evident with the increasing employment of psychologists as counselors. Since they were among the earliest counseling psychologists in Australia, for models of practice they tended to look to overseas universities where this profession was better developed. They also asserted an ethic of overriding professional autonomy in determining how they went about their jobs. In many services testing, study skills and guidance started to disappear, replaced by personal counseling and therapy. Directiveness was eschewed in the enthusiasm for Carl Rogers, his techniques and radical beliefs in the self-directing and self-healing processes in the client (Rogers, 1951). With many new approaches to counseling being developed and competing for attention, the 1970s were exciting times in counseling psychology, the world over. Client centeredness, psychodynamicism, the human potential movement, rational emotive therapy, behavioral methods, and systemic family therapy all attracted their adherents among Australian counselors. Higher education counseling services, with their clientele of intelligent, articulate, minimally disturbed young adults, were seen as ideal places to put the new therapies into practice.

Another strong influence that began to gain sway was the example of student affairs departments in American universities and their role in fostering extracurricular and wider personal development of students. Attracted by this broader vision of what student services might achieve, Australian counselors began to define for themselves this additional campus role of responsibility for the personal development of students during their university years. Influential too, in this regard, was the publication of *Student Counselling in Practice* by the counselors of the British University of Keele (Newsome et al., 1973). This work articulated a clear rationale for the educative role of counselors. Their mission was to provide a process of social and affective education in the university, as an adjunct to the strictly cognitive one offered in the academic programs. Australian counseling services responded to these influences by initiating group programs on such topics as sexuality, assertiveness, and social skills and, in some cases, actually changing the names of their services to include Student Development. Encounter groups designed to identify the clown or comic person within were among other opportunities offered to students to advance their self-knowledge and development.

Generally, counselors were becoming vociferous in their rejection of what they regarded as a band-aid model of simple provision of remedial services. This attitude was made clear in the recommendations of a working party on student services for CAEs in the state of Victoria in 1980. The basis of this report was the cube representation of counselor functioning developed by Morrill, Oetting, and Hurst (1974). Incorporating targets, purposes, and methods of counselor interventions, the cube elegantly conceptualized the multifaceted role that Australian counselors were defining for themselves and legitimized in a sense their increasing concern to engage in developmental and now preventative interventions, no longer limited to students.

In order to reduce the flow of what they perceived as student casualties of the educational system, counselors were turning their attention to their universities and colleges. They saw themselves as champions of the students and, in some situations, took a frankly adversarial stance in relation to the rest of the university. The remote physical location of some counseling services reflected this distancing, particularly from the central administration. At conferences and workshops with other student services colleagues, some were polishing a view of themselves as "boundary-riders" on the edge of their institutions, sounding the alarm about institutional problems.[2] They were to be the agents for change to improve the "climate" and "health" of their universities and colleges. It seems ironic that counseling services, initially established by government to assist the adaptation of students to university, were by 1980 defining their role as one of changing the universities to better adapt to the students.

The Roe Report and Counseling Services

When Roe and his team reported on counseling services in 1982, they described a hard-working, vocal, and sometimes discontented group of professionals, who were attempting to take on new self-defined responsibilities without providing convincing evidence, they noted, of shedding existing ones. Governmental and institutional expectations seemed to have withered into attitudes of indifference or neglect, and the report was critical of the virtual policy vacuum in which student services, including counseling services, operated. Under these circumstances, it was argued, professional autonomy had come to substitute for policy. This was a dangerous trend entailing risks of conflict, irrelevance, burnout, and a slide into indulgence of professional fads and preferences.

Counselors' aspirations to engage in developmental and preventative rather than remedial activities were verbalized very strongly to the survey team, but the report noted a substantial gap between the ideal and the reality. The reality was that most counselors surveyed actually spent most of their time helping students with problems and difficulties.

Aspirations were not plans, it was pointed out, and Roe strongly urged that the only solution to such dilemmas was for student services and their employing institutions to embark on appropriate processes of planning and policy formulation. They also reported a predominant concern among students surveyed for assistance with study and other explicitly educational problems. Although this was an important element in the government's original mandate for counseling services, the Roe team discovered great variety in the extent to which counselors chose to work in this area, many avoiding it altogether. The report questioned whether counselors, who at this stage were mostly trained in psychology and frequently not at all in education, were equipped to do so anyway.

Issues in the Most Recent Decade

If counseling services were born in the 1950s and 1960s, the Roe report could be said to have captured their energetic, idealistic, but confused adolescence. To extend the metaphor, the last decade could certainly be characterized as one of more sober growth toward maturity. The skills, enthusiasms, and aspirations of the 1970s have been tamed and consolidated into a model of professional practice, responsive more to local realities and less to external influences and examples. Various factors were responsible for this development. The Roe report and the controversy and reflection that it prompted certainly represented one factor. Others were the constantly changing educational environment to which the services had to adapt and, it must be stressed, the increased professionalism of the counselors themselves.

Australia's declining economic fortunes in the late 1980s have brought about more sober times generally in higher education. The Commonwealth government has intervened massively in the system in order to make it more cost effective, productive, and accountable. Counseling services have had to absorb their share of cutbacks and have had no choice but to engage in careful priority setting. They have had to formulate policy directions and plans and to bring them into closer articulation with the goals of institutions. Accountability demands have dictated that counselors embrace the language and processes of program evaluation and performance indicators, and they have been struggling to learn these new skills.

Changing demographics in the student population have brought about another enormous change in the educational environment. While the population expansion of the 1950s was based on the meritocratic philosophy that the talented must be identified and educated, changes in the 1980s were basically guided by the social justice principle that everyone should have access to higher education. Barriers to access attributable to gender, disability, and racial, cultural, or social background are to be removed. While implementation lags somewhat behind the ideal, nevertheless counseling services have been confronted by assistance-seeking clients who have very specific needs and gaps in their preparedness for education and whose poverty backgrounds make participation in education a constant struggle. Furthermore, the growing number of students from immigrant backgrounds has been joined by an accelerating influx of fee-paying international students, thereby creating a client population drawn from cultures in which the Western professional counseling process is unknown. Finding ways to assist these students has been perhaps the biggest challenge faced by higher education counselors over the past decade.

That they have successfully risen to the challenge is evidence of their increased skillfulness. By the 1980s graduate training programs in counseling psychology were well established and were producing counselors who had distilled from their exposure to the variety of counseling approaches a solid repertoire of intervention skills. This experience enabled them to work more effectively with clients and gave them an eclectic therapeutic base from which to innovate new strategies to assist the new clients who confronted them. It has been suggested that this positive eclectic approach of Australian counselors represents a movement toward an indigenous theoretical development (Khan, 1983).

The counselors' previous tendency to define new responsibilities for themselves disappeared in the 1980s. While the pressure of shrinking resources and an expanding client population must be held largely responsible, it also seems likely that the counselors' increased assurance and therapeutic effectiveness have played a part by increasing their satisfaction with their basic job of assisting students. The fierce dichotomy they drew between remediation and development has disappeared, and they seem to be working comfortably in a model that subsumes the two. Developmental programs continue as an important part of the work of most services, but these days they are more likely to be linked to students' academic concerns and anxieties about getting employment, for example team-building skills for working in project teams, shyness groups to improve seminar participation, and self-presentation skills for employment interviews.

Student services never did embrace the full student affairs model, and wider extracurricular and more general personal development activities remained where they belonged, the responsibility of the student organizations on campuses.

These days few counselors take an adversarial stance in relation to their institutions. A senior student services administrator has pointed out that this uncomfortable position was perhaps the result of a client-centered professional ethic, focused exclusively on the student as the client (Croker, 1988). This administrator urged that student services reassess this ethic and broaden its view of the client to embrace the whole institution in which it works. This has been gradually taking place.

Mainstreaming has now replaced boundary-riding as the preferred metaphor for locating student services in general.[3] Thus, counselors now seek to be regarded as collaborators in the central academic processes of their institutions. They contribute their professional skills and unique knowledge of students to the decision-making bodies in their institutions and invite consultation with academic staff. Although their goals are always linked with the well-being of students, they assume a professional rather than a partial stance, and, where possible, they leave raw advocacy of a student's point of view to the student unions and organizations.

CURRENT ISSUES AND FUTURE DIRECTIONS

Shrinking Resources and Accountability

The issue of shrinking resources coinciding with increased demands from a more varied and needy population is clearly going to be a serious and continuing one for counseling services in higher education in Australia. Demands for funding justification and accountability are increasing, and framing an appropriate response is inherently difficult. Peterson and Burck (1982, 17:35) expressed it well:

> How can an accountability system be established that credits human services workers fairly for what they can and cannot accomplish when the results of human intervention are often ill-defined, inter-active and unpredictable; cost-accounting procedures varied and often simplistic; and the causal linkages between resources and results tenuous at best?

The Roe report (1982) suggested that student services accept the notion that justification will always be difficult and risky and that they simply represent an act of faith by their institutions. Unfortunately, in the Australian educational environment of the 1990s, faith is another shrinking commodity. It is essential that counselors develop the skills of strategic planning and evaluation and find ways of demonstrating their contribution to the achievement of their institutions' goals. There is evidence that they are beginning to do so (Quintrell et al., 1989; Robertson, 1990).

Learning Skills

The new student populations are exhibiting an unprecedented need for assistance in developing academic skills to cope with higher education. This is particularly true of international students who need to adjust to an academic environment that is frequently very different from that in their home countries. Over the past decade, counseling services have increasingly reassumed responsibility for learning skills. Indeed, as they have focused their missions more closely on the academic goals of their institutions, it has been unavoidable, and those services that have most successfully mainstreamed tend to have been those perceived by their institutions as contributing valuable assistance to the learning process. But caution is necessary in determining how much responsibility for this area rests with counselors and how much with academic departments. Unchecked, this demand could overwhelm services. Furthermore, the point raised by the Roe report is still relevant: counselor training courses are still psychologically oriented, and counselors with the necessary additional training in education are still scarce.

Research

Counseling psychology in Australia has been characterized as a very practice-oriented profession (Penney, 1981) that assigns a low priority to research (Schoen, 1986). Higher education counselors, however, have taken a prominent role in the research and publication record that exists, with counselors at the University of New South Wales and the University of Sydney playing leading roles. In leaner times, research inevitably becomes a lower priority for services. Ironically, however, it is under these circumstances that investigations into client needs and characteristics and evaluation of interventions become essential in ensuring the best possible allocation of resources. How to continue to perform the research necessary to the proper delivery of a professional service when resources are limited is a very real challenge for higher education counselors of the 1990s.

PROFESSIONAL IDENTITY AND TRAINING

Counseling has not developed as a profession in its own right in Australia as it has done in Britain and the United States. Social workers have had some claims to employment in the field, but increasingly psychologists have come to dominate it. Now, professional training in counseling is inevitably at graduate level in counseling psychology. The Australian Psychological Society has determined that within five years this training will be exclusively at the master's degree level.

There has been a history of debate about the professional identity of Australian counseling psychologists (Penney, 1981; Schoen, 1986; Williams, 1978, 1989; Wills, 1980). The most recent opinion is that of Williams, "that there is still no clear sense of professional identity arising from a common preparation" (1989:15). However, an earlier statement by the same author, "the locations in which counseling psychologists work still contribute to their identity" (1978:35), seems more relevant to higher education counselors. Although this group of counselors is not unaffected by the debates about the distinctions between counselors and counseling psychologists and among psychologists themselves, over the past forty years they have developed a maturing sense of identity based on their involvement and struggle with the educational environment and institutions in which they have worked. Today many of them have attained a more relevant sense of professional belonging as a subgroup of the educational student services than as a subgroup of the psychological profession. Their access to both has certainly enriched their professional lives.

CAREER OPPORTUNITIES

As a career, higher education counseling in Australia in the 1990s is available only to counseling psychologists who have completed postgraduate professional training approved by the Australian Psychological Society. It is a popular area of employment, and there is keen competition for the available jobs among the growing pool of appropriately trained people. Because employment is linked to Commonwealth government educational and fiscal policies, it is susceptible to cutbacks when national budgets are tightened. This is currently the situation.

CONCLUSION

Skilled, aware, adaptable to change, and committed to assisting students to achieve their goals, counselors are valuable professionals on the campuses of Australian universities and colleges. Certainly, the educational environment of the 1990s presents them with formidable challenges. But they have adapted, grown, and risen to challenges before, and there is every reason to be confident that they will continue to do so.

NOTES

1. Seventh triennial conference of Australian and New Zealand Student Services Association (ANZSSA), January 1991, Sydney, Australia.
2. Association of Campus Community Services workshop, July 1977, Melbourne, Australia.
3. ANZSSA Heads of Student Services conference, February 1991, Melbourne, Australia.

REFERENCES

Australian Vice-Chancellors Committee (AVCC). (1960). *Report of a Conference on University Education.*

Commission on Advanced Education. (1972). *Third Report.* Canberra: AGPS.

Committee on Australian Universities. (1957). *Report.* Canberra: G.P. (Murray Report).

Croker, S. (1988). "Student Services: Can We Justify Our Continued Existence?" Keynote address to the sixth triennial conference of Australian and New Zealand Student Services Association, Auckland, New Zealand.

Khan, J. A. (1983). The evolution of counseling and guidance in Australia: or, as yet no counselling kangaroos? *Personnel and Guidance Journal*, 61, 469–472.

Morrill, W., Oetting, E., and Hurst, J. (1974). Dimensions of counselling functioning. *Personnel and Guidance Journal*, 52, 354–359.

Newsome, A., Thorne, B. J., and Wyld, K. L. (1973). *Student Counselling in Practice.* London: University of London Press.

Niemann, N. M. (1965). "Each to His Full Stature. The Discovery and Development of Individual Talent: The Role of the Student Counsellor." Paper presented at conference of Australian College of Education, Brisbane, Australia.

Penney, J. F. (1981). The development of counseling psychology in Australia. *Australian Psychologist*, 16, 20–29.

Peterson, G. W., and Burck, H. D. (1982). A competency approach to accountability in human service programs. *Personnel and Guidance Journal*, 17, 34–48.

Quintrell, N., McMullen, D., and Nixon, S. (1989). Evaluating student services. *ANZSSA News*, 33, 1–13.

Robertson, M. F. (1990). Programme planning and evaluation in a counselling service. Paper presented at the second conference of the Asia Pacific Student Services Association, Kuala Lumpur, Malaysia.

Roe, E., Foster, G., Moses, I., Sanker, M., and Storey, P. (1982). *A Report on Student Services in Tertiary Education in Australia.* Commonwealth Tertiary Education Commission, Evaluative Studies Program, Tertiary Education Institute, University of Queensland.

Rogers, C. R. (1951). *Client Centered Therapy*. Boston: Houghton Mifflin Co.

Schoen, L. G. (1986). The development of counseling psychology in Australia. *Australian Psychologist*, 16, 20–29.

Universities Commission. (1975). *Sixth Report*. Canberra: AGPS.

Williams, C. (1978). The dilemma of counselling psychology. *Australian Psychologist*, 13, 33–40.

Williams, C. (1989). What is distinctive about counselling psychology? *Australian Counselling Psychologist*, 5, 15–19.

Wills, G. (1980). An examination of the relationship between counselling and counselling psychology. *Australian Psychologist*, 15, 73–84.

9. Counseling in the Asia-Pacific Region: Challenges and Strategies

ABDUL HALIM OTHMAN
AMIR AWANG

Asia, the world's largest continent, with almost 60 percent of the world's population, provides a fertile ground for the development of diverse cultures, languages, and religions. The Pacific Ocean, which spans four continents, provides an even greater diversity of peoples and cultures. We do not propose to deal with all these diversities in the discussion of the phenomena related to counseling in the Asia-Pacific region. Suffice it to say, however, that the presence of these complex phenomena as illustrated in the countries we have presented in this volume will provide some insights into the many problems and challenges facing Asian-Pacific counselors.

Much of what we present in this chapter stems from our own experiences and observations of the phenomena that exist in Malaysia. However, after reading what our counterparts have written about their own experiences, we are beginning to see some interesting similarities and some differences, which somewhat strengthen our belief that certain human experiences are shared across national frontiers.

What are some of the major problems and challenges that Asian-Pacific counselors, in particular Asian counselors, are facing and will likely be facing in the future? How do they cope with some of these challenges? These are among the questions that will intrigue us for some time in our careers. We would like to propose that among some of the major pressing problems confronting counseling and counselors in the region are

- The counselor identity crisis
- The drug menace and other social problems
- The degeneration of moral and ethical values
- The coping behavior and skill to meet the ever increasing stress resulting from development and progress
- The breakdown of the extended family system and the breakup of families.

THE COUNSELOR IDENTITY CRISIS

Traditionally, Asians have coped with their problems through consultation and advice and the "guidance" received from traditional healers. This tradition still exists, and many Asians continue to resort to traditional healers. Their faith in the ability of these healers alone constitutes a major element of success in treatment.

Present-day counselors, who are much oriented toward the more structured and more scientifically based approaches to healing, initially had to accept the reality of time. In urban areas the new approaches are much more readily accepted. The greatest threat, perhaps, comes from the lack of acknowledgment that counseling is a professional activity that requires not only adequate but also recognized and well-supervised training. Currently, the term *counselor* seems to be used very freely and very loosely. Everyone, even those with minimum counseling knowledge and skill, prefers to be acknowledged as a counselor. The net consequence of such a situation is not only a dilution of the professional standard, but worse, confusion among the end-users of services. In fact, poorly delivered services by inadequately trained counselors may be a disservice to the growing profession of counseling and may even lead to a loss of confidence in counseling services.

Consequently, we strongly believe that the time is long overdue for us to professionally define the professional counselor and obtain government and necessary legal backing to avoid these dangers. This objective is justified on the basis that our clients deserve professional care for their mental and psychological well-being and so their welfare must be protected. Such concerns were generally felt in many countries around the region, with some more successful in overcoming them than others. In Japan, counseling is dominated by clinical psychologists, whereas in Australia counselors are registered psychologists. Counselors in some other countries have yet to define their boundaries.

DRUG MENACE AND OTHER SOCIAL PROBLEMS

Drug addiction and drug dependency among people in the fifteen to thirty-five-year-old group have become rampant, in spite of both governmental and nongovernmental efforts. Much of the earlier work has been remedial, but of late efforts also have been channeled toward preventative and developmental programs. Many national resources have been targeted for the care of these drug-dependent people. Both internal and external factors have been associated with drug dependency. For example, in Singapore and Malaysia counseling as a preventative enterprise developed from the overriding concern with drug addiction in the two countries. Counselors have a very big responsibility here, particularly in the preventative, remedial, and developmental areas. The question before us is: are counselors adequately trained to handle all these areas? Drug addicts are well known for their uncooperative and defensive responses.

As counselors we generally have the necessary knowledge and skills to assist normal people to develop, although some peripheral cases of abnormality are within our jurisdiction. The drug problem is a social menace, requiring different treatment approaches.

DEGENERATION OF MORAL AND
ETHICAL VALUES

Asians have traditionally been admired and respected for their strong adherence to moral and ethical values in decision making and action. They are generally other-directed, in the sense that they always consider what others think and feel. Chiu observed that the Chinese culture is morally referenced. Ethical and moral value have become part of the Asian conscience.

Recently, the importance of these values seems to have shifted. Many Asians are becoming more individualistic and materialistic. Ever more decisions are being made, and actions taken, without adequate consideration for moral and ethical values and for the group and individual conscience. Observations of this lack or absence of conscience have become common; this lack is disturbing for it can bring about unpredictable behaviors among the present generation. Counseling can play an important role in reinstating this lost conscience and the coveted ethical and moral values ingrained in Asian cultures, thereby restoring the harmony and peace of the societies.

COPING BEHAVIOR TO MEET THE
EVER INCREASING STRESS

Another visible phenomenon sweeping across Asia and the Pacific region is the rat race. Because of several socioeconomic factors, more and more people are being subjected to increasing stress in their daily lives. The World Health Organization has reported an increasing number of deaths resulting from hypertension, heart attacks, and nervous breakdowns. Even Type B personalities are not spared this tragic destiny.

The extended family unit which previously served as a useful support to individual family members is rapidly disappearing. Social mobility and urban migration have taken members of the family away from their original homes. Thrown into the urban rat race, members of the rural population who migrate to the cities cannot adjust quickly enough to the tempo and rhythm of the urban culture. This has led to serious stress and tension. The effects of modernization and improved technology are currently being felt by newly developed countries such as Singapore and Malaysia. The problem has grown in magnitude with every rural-urban migration that services the booming industrial and business sectors in the cities.

The school system has not been able to cope with this adjustment. Within the Asian context, a large proportion of the school children drop out of school after about nine years of schooling. Truancy and school leaving have not been a phenomenon solely in industrialized countries like Japan and Korea but also in the newly emerging industrialized economies like Malaysia and Singapore. These school dropouts will constitute a major group of young and problem-ridden adolescents and will be a tremendous loss to the society. Adolescents are normally torn between their status as children and young adults, creating a lot of psychological pressure for adults.

Those who succeed in school will also be caught up in the ever demanding and sometimes unhealthy paper chase. In Japan, Korea, Australia, Singapore, and Malaysia, pressure for academic and intellectual success has led to serious stress among students who cannot cope, resulting in a need for increased counseling and other support activities in schools and colleges. Very often parental expectations create undue pressure on young children. Without the extended family support and without the ability to cope, the stress they experience will continue to increase until some form of release is found. How can counseling and guidance be of service to these groups of stressful people—the young adults and the floating young adolescents?

BREAKDOWN OF THE EXTENDED FAMILY SYSTEM

As briefly mentioned earlier, the extended family system which used to be a useful asset for the Asian people is now breaking down and doing so rapidly. Sociocultural and economic factors have significantly contributed to this breakdown. It is not uncommon for the present-day generation not to know other relatives beyond the immediate family. Unfortunately, this breakdown has taken away with it the support of persons to confide in and of confidants with whom one can share life's stresses.

As a consequence, society is now looking to counselors and other helping agents for support. Counselors are expected to play significant and effective roles as parent surrogates, at the same time as they are bogged down with countless other responsibilities. The presence of counselors in some parts of this region has not been legally and adequately acknowledged and endorsed by the relevant authorities. However, accreditation and licensing of counselors have been implemented in countries such as Australia, Japan, and Korea. New Zealand, Malaysia, Singapore, and Indonesia apparently have no regulations governing counseling practice, a situation that somewhat hinders efforts to deliver services in the most effective and efficient manner.

How can we as counselors help fill the vacuum created by the breakdown of the extended family system?

EFFECTIVE COUNSELING AND GUIDANCE SERVICES

In schools, guidance services are generally considered the equivalent of pupil personnel services, and have been in great demand recently. The need to pursue appropriate education and to make suitable vocational choices is becoming increasingly conspicuous. The present-day generation has become more selective of the courses they would like to study and the vocations they want to pursue. The rapid socioeconomic and technological development of the present and future will inevitably compound their problems in career decision making.

Existing systems, be they public or private, have not adequately provided the much needed services, not because the need is not recognized or felt, but rather because trained personnel are not available in large numbers.

If we are committed to the belief that right choices can and will, to a large extent, determine future success as proposed by John Holland and Donald Super, for instance, then we have an obligation to ensure that effective guidance services be available. We might have to summon all possible influences to achieve this end. Outside the educational system there is also a dire need for increased counseling and human services either in the organizations, industry, or business. Developments in Malaysia, Korea, Singapore, Australia, and elsewhere in the region where counseling has responded to the needs of industry, commerce, the military, and public services augurs well for the future of the profession in those countries.

INDIGENOUS COUNSELING IN ASIA

It is the dream of every Asian counselor to witness the emergence of indigenous counseling theories, techniques, practices, and approaches. It is indeed a noble and a natural dream. We believe that indigenous counseling will be more appropriate to meet the local needs of the Asian and Pacific peoples.

The different cultural and psychological orientations of Asians and minorities in New Zealand and other places, as compared to Westerners, as highlighted by Chiu, Sato, Yeo, Henshaw, and others in this book, clearly suggest the need for the development of indigenous counseling systems in this region.

It is not easy to say where we are now in our endeavor to achieve this objective, but clearly we need to build theories on solid empirical data and evidence, which to our mind, are still inadequate. There is now a strong need for a more focused, more collaborative research before we are anywhere near the target. The atmosphere is quite ripe for progress in this area. More and more graduates, teachers, and educationists are keen to pursue higher studies. We should capitalize on and, if necessary, positively exploit the current interest to move our dream a step nearer the sought-after reality.

Although there are international professional organizations such as the Association of Psychological and Educational Counselors of Asia (APECA), the Asia-Pacific Student Services Association (APSSA), the Afro-Asian Psychological Association (AAPA), or the Association of Southeast Asian Institutions of Higher Learning (ASAIHL), more positive roles can be played by counselors in the Asia-Pacific region to indigenize counseling.

Selected References

Angel, R., and Thoits, P. (1987). The impact of culture on the cognitive structure of illness. *Culture, Medicine and Psychiatry*, 11, 465–494.

Association of Japanese Clinical Psychology. (1988). *The Manual for the Candidate of Clinical Psychologist*. Tokyo: Seishinshobo.

Awang, Amir, and Mirasa, Latiff. (1984). Guidance and counseling in Malaysian schools. A review and critique. In *Proceedings of Third Asian Workshop on Child and Adolescent Development*. (Vol. 2, pp. 1–18.) Kuala Lumpur: Universiti Malaya.

Aubrey, F. (1982). A house divided: guidance and counseling in 20th century. *Personnel and Guidance Journal*, 61 (4), 198–204.

Beek, M. V. (1987). *Konseling Pastoral* [Pastoral counseling]. Semarang, Indonesia: Satya Wacana.

Bradley, M. K. (1978). Counseling past and present: is there a future? *Personnel and Guidance Journal*, 57, 42–45.

Brown, W. F. (1974). Effectiveness of paraprofessionals: the evidence. *Personnel and Guidance Journal*, 53 (4), 257–264.

Byun, C. J., and Choo, S. H. (1980). A communication skills training program for high school peer counselors. *Journal of Student Guidance* (Kyungpook National University), 13, 1–85 (in Korean).

Byun, C. J., and Kim, S. H. (1980). An assertiveness training program. *Journal of Student Guidance* (Kyungpook National University), 13, 51–85 (in Korean).

Cheng, C. K. (1946). Characteristic traits of the Chinese people. *Social Forces*, 25, 146–155.

Chiam, H. K. (1987). *Adolescents in Malaysia*. Paper presented at the Seminar on Education for Peace, Human Understanding and Development, World Organization of Scout Movement, Kuala Lumpur, Malaysia.

Chinese Culture Connection (1987). Chinese values and the search for culture-free dimensions of culture. *Journal of Cross-Cultural Psychology*, 18 (2), 143–164.

Departemen Pendidikan dan Kebudayaan RI. (1976). *Kurikulum Pedoman Bimbingan dan Penyuluhan di Sekolah* [Curriculum guide to school guidance and counseling]. Buku III.C, Jakarta: Balai Pustaka.

Drum, D. J., and Figler, H. E. (1976). *Outreach in Counseling*. Cranston, R.I.: Carroll Press.

Eisenberg, L. (1981). The social context of health: effects of time, place and person. In Stuart H. Fine, Robert Krell, and Tsung-yi Lin (eds.), *Today's Priorities in Mental Health: Children and Families—Needs, Rights, and Action* (35). London: D. Reidel Publishing Co.

Goffman, E. (1955). On face-work: an analysis of ritual elements in social interaction. *Psychiatry*, 18, 213–231.

Goodyear, R. K. (1976). Counselors as community psychologists. *Personnel and Guidance Journal*, 54, 512–516.

Hermansson, G. (1990). It won't be long: Counselling and guidance poised for the nineties. In John Small and Tony Ambrose (eds.), *Counselling and Guidance Towards the Nineties*. Palmerston North: New Zealand Counselling and Guidance Association.

Herr, E. L. (1985). AACD: An association committed to unity through diversity. *Journal of Counseling and Development*, 63, 395–404.

Hidano, S. (1989). Present society and counseling. *Japanese Journal of Counseling Science*, 22, 1–2.

Hofstede, G. (1980). *Culture's Consequences: International Differences in Work-related Value*. London and Beverly Hills, Calif.: Sage.

Hofstede, G. (1983). Dimensions of national cultures in fifty countries and three regions. In J. B. Deregowski, S. Dziurawiec, and R. C. Annis (eds.), *Explications in Cross-cultural Psychology*, pp. 335–355. Lisse, Netherlands: Swets and Zeitlinger.

Hong, K. J. (1986). *Guidance for Growth*. Seoul: Tam Gu Dang (in Korean).

Hsieh, T. T., Shybut, J., and Lotsof, E. J. et al. (1969). Internal versus external control and ethnic group membership: a cross-cultural comparison. *Journal of Consulting and Clinical Psychology*, 33 (1), 122–124.

Hui, C. H., and Villareal, M. J. (1989). Individualism-collectivism and psychological needs: their relationships in two cultures. *Journal of Cross-Cultural Psychology*, 20 (3), 17–23.

Humphreys, J. A., Traxler, A. E., and North, R. D. (1960). *Guidance Services*. Chicago: Science Research Associates, Inc.

Ibrahim, A., Helms, J., and Thompson, Donald L. (1983). Counselor role and function: an approach by consumer and counselor. *Personnel and Guidance Journal*, 61–64, 597–601.

Ivey, A. B. (1983). *Intentional Interviewing and Counseling*. Monterey, Calif.: Brooks/Cole Publishing Co.

Jackson, R., and Juniper, D. F. (1971). *A Manual of Educational Guidance*. London: Holt, Rinehart and Winston Ltd.

Kahn, H. (1979). *World Economic Development: 1979 and Beyond*. London: Croom Helm.

Khan, J. A. (1983). The evolution of counseling and guidance in Australia: or, as yet no counselling kangaroos? *Personnel and Guidance Journal*, 61, 469–472.

Kim, N. O. (1987). A study skill training program. I: Reading skills. *Journal of Student Guidance* (Kyungpook National University), 20, 57–87 (in Korean).

Lee, C. H. (1982). *Introduction to Counseling*. Seoul: Park Yong Sa Publishing Co. (in Korean).

Lee, H. D. (1982a). The recent trends and theoretical background in guidance and counseling. *Guidance and Counseling* (Keimyung University), 7, 1–17 (in Korean).

Lee, H. D. (1982b). *Human Relations Training*. Seoul: Joong Ang Juk Sung Chool Pan Sa (in Korean).

Lee, J. C. (1988). *Guidance*. Seoul: Moon Um Sa Publishing Co. (in Korean).

Lee, S. Y. (1984). A values clarification program. *Guidance and Counseling* (Keimyung University), 9, 49–76 (in Korean).

Lee, Y. D., and Chung, W. S. (1962). *Principles and Practices of Guidance*. Seoul: Kyo Yuk Kwa Hak Sa (in Korean).

Leong, Y. C., Chiam, H. K., and Chew, S. M. (eds.). (1984). Proceedings of the Workshop on Preparation for Adulthood. Third Asian Workshop on Child and Adolescent Development, April 9–14, 1984. Kuala Lumpur: Faculty of Education, University of Malaya.

Lewis, J. A., and Lewis, M. D. (1977). *Community Counseling: A Human Services Approach*. New York: John Wiley and Sons.

Lin, T., and Lin, M. (1978). Service-delivery issues in Asian North American Communities. *American Journal of Psychiatry*, 135, 344–453.

Lloyd, A. (1987). Counselor education in Malaysia. *Counselor Education and Supervision*, 26 (3), 221–227.

Lloyd, A. (1988). The sources of citations for guidance and counseling articles. *Jurnal PERKAMA*, 2, 29–38.

Mapiare, A. (1984). *Pengantar Bimbingan dan Konseling di Sekolah* [An introduction of guidance and counseling in schools]. Surabaya, Indonesia: Penerbit Usaha Nasional.

Ministry of Education, Malaysia. (1961). Perlantikan Guru Bimbingan, KP/5209/35/(4) [Appointment of guidance teachers]. (Circular Behagian Perancangan dan Penyelidikan Pelajaran).

Ministry of Education, Malaysia. (1963). *Guidance Services*. Kuala Lumpur: Kementerian Pelajaran, Malaysia.

Ministry of Education, Malaysia. (1968). *Outline of Guidance Services*. Kuala Lumpur: Behagian Perancangan dan Penyelidikan Pelajaran.

Ministry of Education, Malaysia. (1970). *Education in Malaysia*. Kuala Lumpur: Dewan Bahasa Dan Pustaka.

Ministry of Education, Malaysia. (1979). *Report of the Cabinet Committee: To Review the Implementation of the Education Policy*. Kuala Lumpur: Berita Publishing Sdn. Bhd.

Morrill, W., Oetting, E., and Hurst, J. (1974). Dimensions of counselling functioning. *Personnel and Guidance Journal*, 52, 354–359.

Murase, T. (1990). For next ten years. *Journal of Japanese Clinical Psychology*, 9, 2.

Naisbitt, J., and Aburdene, P. (1990). *Megatrends 2000* (FX Budiyanto, trans.). Jakarta, Indonesia: Binapura Aksara.

Nakamura, H. (1988). The past, present and the future about Japanese counseling science. *Japanese Journal of Counseling Science*, 21, 1.

Newsome, A., Thorne, B. J., and Wyld, K. L. (1973). *Student Counseling in Practice*. London: University of London Press Ltd.

Niemann, N. M. (1965). The role of the student counsellor. Paper presented at conference of Australian College of Education, Brisbane, Australia.

Nugent, F. A. (1981). *Professional Counseling*. Monterey, Calif.: Brooks/Cole Publications.

Okubo, Y. (1990). In future of clinical psychologists. *Bulletin of Japan Society of Certified Clinical Psychologist*, 1, 1.

Okubo, Y. (1990). *Human Mind* (vol. 33). Japan: Hyoronsha.

Othman, Abdul Halim. (1984). Peranan kaunselor di sekolah dalam konteks perubahan masyarakat [The role of school counselors in the context of societal changes]. *Majallah Psikologi*, 5, 44–50.

Othman, Abdul Halim. (1984). Penyelidikan Kaunseling dan Bimbingan di Malaysia: Satu penerokaan di sebuah institusi pengajian tinggi [Research in counseling and guidance in Malaysia: explorations in an institution of higher education]. *Jurnal PERKAMA*, 1, 122–139.

Othman, A. H., and Awang, A. (1990 May). Counseling in Asia: Challenges and Strategies for the 1990's. Paper presented at Eighth APECA Biennial Conference Workshop, Pulau Pinang, Malaysia.

Othman, Abdul Halim, and Rahman, Wan Rafaei Abdul. (1987). Issues and problems related to the teaching of psychology and training of psychologists. *The Role of Universities in Developing Nations*. Bangi: UKM.

Othman, Abdul Halim, Rahman, Wan Rafaei Abdul, and Nasir, Rohany. (1981). *Kaunseling Dan Kerjaya*. Working paper presented at the Second Seminar Psikologi Dan Masyarakat Ke-2, April 20–23, 1981, Universiti Kebangsaan Malaysia, Bangi.

Othman, Abdul Halim, Rahman, Wan Rafaei Abdul, and Yusof, Aminuddin. (1983). An evaluation of the first diploma in counseling program at the Universiti Kebangsaan Malaysia. *Akademika*, 23, 83–95.

Paris, C. (1979). *The Counselor as Change Agent*. Ann Arbor, Mich.: Eric Counseling and Personnel Services Clearinghouse.

Park, S. S. (1986). *Guidance*. Seoul: Chung Min Sa Publishing Co. (in Korean).

Penney, J. F. (1981). The development of counseling psychology in Australia. *Australian Psychologist*, 16, 20–29.

Peterson, G. W., and Burck, H. D. (1982). A competency approach to accountability in human service programs. *Personnel and Guidance Journal*, 17, 34–48.

Prayitno. (1987). *Professionalisasi Konseling dan Pendidikan Konselor* [Professionalization of counseling and counselor education]. Jakarta: Dirjen Dikti Proyek Pengembangan Lembaga Pendidikan Tenaga Kependidikan.

Quintrell, N., McMullen, D., and Nixon, S. (1989). Evaluating student services. *ANZSSA News*, 33, 1–13.

Rogers, C. R. (1951). *Client Centered Therapy*. Boston: Houghton Mifflin Co.

Schoen, L. G. (1986). The development of counseling psychology in Australia. *Australian Psychologist*, 16, 20–29.

Scorzelli, J. F. (1987). Counseling in Malaysia: an emerging profession. *Journal of Counseling and Development*, 65, 238–240.

Scorzelli, J. F. (1987). Counselor education in Malaysia: a need for a rehabilitation specialisation. *Jurnal Perkama*, 2, 53–58.

Seol, K. M. (1990). A group counseling program for increasing personal happiness. *Research Review* (Dong-A University), 19, 45–65 (in Korean).

Surya, M. (1988). *Dasar-Dasar Konseling Pendidikan (Teori & Concept)* [Introduction to educational counseling—theory and concept]. Yogyakarta: Kota Kembang.

Talmun, M. (1991). *Single Session Therapy*. San Francisco: Jossey-Bass Publishers.

Tan, T. H. (1979). Emotional problems of adolescents. *Jernal Panduan MAVOGA*, 1, 39–45.

T.H.E. Project. (1975). A student development model for student affairs in tomorrow's education. *Journal of College Student Personnel*, 16, 334–341.

Tindall, J. A. (1989). *Peer Counseling: An In-Depth Look at Training Peer Helpers* (3rd ed.). Muncie, Ind.: Accelerated Development Inc.

Tseng, W. S. (1978). Traditional and modern psychiatric care in Taiwan. In A. Kleinman (ed.), *Culture and Healing in Asian Countries: Anthropological, Psychiatric and Public Health*. New York: Cambridge University Press.

Uchiyama, K. (1984). *Counseling*. Nihon Bunkakagakusya.

Webster, A. C., and Hermansson, G. L. (1983). Guidance and counseling in New Zealand. *Personnel and Guidance Journal*, 61 (8), 472–475.

Wing, R. L. (1986). *The Tao of Power*. Wellingborough, Northamptonshire: Aquarian Press.

Winterbourn, R. (1974). *Guidance Services in New Zealand Education*. Wellington: New Zealand Council for Educational Research.

Williams, C. (1978). What is distinctive about counselling psychology? *Australian Counselling Psychologist*, 5, 15–19.

Wills, G. (1980). An examination of the relationship between counselling and counselling psychology. *Australian Psychologist*, 15, 73–84.

Wilson, H., and Rotter, C. (1982). School counseling: a look into the future. *Personnel and Guidance Journal*, 60 (6), 353–357.

Yeo, A. (1990). Developments and trends of counseling in Singapore—a personal view. *Asian Bulletin of Counselling*, 1, 1.

Yoon, H. S., and Lee, H. D. (1980). A learning program for personal growth. *Guidance and Counseling* (Keimyung University), 1–46 (in Korean).

Index

About the Contributors

Amir Awang, Professor of Counseling Psychology and Deputy Vice-chancellor (Student Affairs), Science University of Malaysia. Professor Awang was President of the Malaysian Counseling Association and the Association of Psychological and Educational Counsellors of Asia. He writes counseling and psychology books in Malay.

Sharifah Bee Aboo Bakar, Lecturer, Federation Teachers College, Penang. Bakar completed a degree in history and, later, diplomas in education and psychology (counseling) and a master's degree in guidance and counseling.

Herbert Chiu, Senior Lecturer, Division of Humanities and Social Science, City Polytechnic of Hong Kong. He has worked in school counseling and has published *Becoming a Father* and other articles on mental health.

Margaret E. Henshaw, Student Counselor at the University of Waikato, New Zealand. Henshaw works with international students and students with disabilities and is an active member of the Australia New Zealand Student Services Association (ANZSSA) and the Asia-Pacific Student Services Association.

Hyung Deuk Lee, Professor, Department of Education, Keimyung University, Korea. Professor Lee is a Counseling Psychologist certified by the Korean Psychological Association. He is president of the Korean Association of Developmental Counseling and has published several books, including *Practice of Group Counseling*.

J. T. Lobby Loekmono, Lecturer and Director of Counseling Center at the Satya Wacana Christian University, Indonesia. Currently on leave to complete the Ph.D. at the Science University, Malaysia, he is an active member of the Asian Psychological and Educational Counselors Association.

Abdul Halim Othman, Professor of Counseling Psychology. Professor Othman is President of the Malaysian Psychological Association and former President of the Malaysian Counseling Association. His major interests include counselor education, student development research, and cross-cultural counseling. He is Chief Editor of three Malaysian journals and Editorial Advisor to the *International Journal for the Advancement of Counseling* and *Indian Journal of Personality and Clinical Studies*.

Margaret Robertson, Psychologist. Robertson has worked in educational counseling and guidance at both the secondary and university levels for 22 years. She is currently Head of the Counseling Service at the Royal Melbourne Institute of Technology. She has published regularly in the *International Journal for the Advancement of Counseling*.

Mika Saito, Lecturer in Counseling Psychology. Saito holds an M.A. in Counseling and is an active member of the Asian Psychological and Educational Counselors Association.

Ki Moon Seol, Professor, Department of Education, Dong-A University, Korea. Professor Seol is a Counseling Psychologist certified by the Korean Psychological Association and translator of American counseling books into Korean.

Anthony Yeo, Director, Counseling and Care Center, Singapore. Yeo specializes in marriage and family therapy and counselor education. He is a Clinical Member of the American Association for Marriage and Family Therapy, and author of *A Helping Hand*, *Living with Stress*, and *Groups Alive*.